NOISE INDUCED HEARING LOSS IN MANUFACTURING INDUSTRIES

HOW MUCH DOES IT COST TO THE WORKERS, FAMILIES AND SOCIETY?

PROFESSOR DR. SYED MOHAMED ALJUNID
NORAITA BINTI TAHIR

PARTRIDGE

Copyright © 2020 by Professor Dr. Syed Mohamed Aljunid Noraita Binti Tahir.

ISBN: Softcover   978-1-5437-5789-7
             eBook   978-1-5437-5790-3

All rights reserved. No part of this book may be used or reproduced by any means, graphic, electronic, or mechanical, including photocopying, recording, taping or by any information storage retrieval system without the written permission of the author except in the case of brief quotations embodied in critical articles and reviews.

Because of the dynamic nature of the Internet, any web addresses or links contained in this book may have changed since publication and may no longer be valid. The views expressed in this work are solely those of the author and do not necessarily reflect the views of the publisher, and the publisher hereby disclaims any responsibility for them.

Print information available on the last page.

To order additional copies of this book, contact
Toll Free 800 101 2657 (Singapore)
Toll Free 1 800 81 7340 (Malaysia)
orders.singapore@partridgepublishing.com

www.partridgepublishing.com/singapore

CONTENTS

Acknowledgement xi

Chapter 1: Introduction 1

  1.1 Study Background 1
  1.2 Research Questions 5
  1.3 Research Scope 7
  1.4 Research Justification 7
  1.5 Objectives Of The Study 9
  1.6 Hypothesis 9

Chapter 2: Literature Review 11

  2.1 Introduction 11
  2.2 Definition Of Noise Induced Hearing Loss 11
  2.3 Type Of Hearing Loss 12
  2.4 Auditory Effects Of Noise Exposure 14
  2.5 Prevalence Of Nihl 16
  2.6 Incidence Of Nihl In Malaysia 18
  2.7 Management Of Occupational Noise Induced
       Hearing Loss Management Overview 19
  2.8 Noise Exposure Regulations 21
      2.8.1 Permissible Exposure Limit (PEL) 22
      2.8.2 Audiometric program & treatment 23
      2.8.3 Control measures 24
      2.8.4 Warning Signs and record keeping 25

2.9 Hearing Healthcare Professionals 25
2.10 Possible Treatment For Hearing Loss 26
2.11 Hearing Conservation Programme And
      Requirements Of The Law 26
2.12 Study On Costs Of Hearing Loss 27
    2.12.1 Direct cost *30*
    2.12.2 Indirect cost *31*
    2.12.3 Economic burden *31*
2.13 Research Conceptual Framework 31

Chapter 3: Research Methodology 34

3.1 Introduction 34
3.2 Study Design 34
3.3 Study Setting And Study Duration 35
3.4 Sampling Frame 36
3.5 Inclusion And Exclusion Criteria 36
3.6 Sample Size 37
3.7 Data Collection Tools 38
3.8 Data Collection For Government 39
3.9 Data Analysis 41
    *3.9.1 Estimation of total number of NIHL cases
      among manufacturing workers* *41*
    3.9.2 Total cost of NIHL *42*
    *3.9.2.1 Estimating the cost of NIHL by workers
      and caregivers* *43*
    3.9.2.2 Estimating the cost of NIHL by employers *43*
    3.6.2.3 Estimating cost of NIHL by government *44*
    3.9.2.4 Estimating the Direct Cost of NIHL *44*
    3.9.2.5 Estimating the Indirect Cost of NIHL *44*
    3.9.2.6 Estimating the Total Cost of NIHL *45*

Chapter 4: Results: Estimation Of NIHL Cases
Among Manufacturing Workers 46

4.1 Introduction 46
4.2 Profiles Of Manufacturing Industries Having
    Workers With NIHL 46
4.3 Demographic Data Of Employers.........................47
4.4 Noise Level Exposure In The Industries 47
4.5 Implementation Of Hearing Conservation
    Program 49
4.6 Estimation Of The Total Number Of NIHL
    Cases Among Manufacturing Workers 50
4.7 Incidence Rate And Risk Of NIHL Cases
    Among Manufacturing Workers............................53

Chapter 5: Results: Cost And Economic Burden Of
Nihl In Manufacturing Industries In Malaysia.... 55

5.1 Introduction 55
5.2 Profiles Of Manufacturing Workers With NIHL 55
5.3 Status Of Treatment And Rehabilitation 58
5.4 Cost Of NIHL...60
5.5 Cost Of Nihl By Workers And Employers...............61
5.6 Cost Of NIHL Borne By The Worker....................62
   5.6.1 Direct Cost Of NIHL Borne By Worker.............62
   5.6.2 Indirect Cost Of NIHL By Worker 63
5.7 Cost Of NIHL Borne By The Employer 64
   5.7.1 Direct cost of NIHL by employer......................64
   5.7.2 Indirect cost of NIHL borne by employer 65
5.8 Cost Of NIHL By Government 66
   5.8.1 Direct cost of NIHL by government..................66
   5.8.2 Indirect cost of NIHL borne by government 67
5.9 Total Economic Burden Of NIHL In Malaysia 68
   5.9.1 Total direct cost of NIHL................................68
   5.9.2 Total indirect cost of NIHL 69

5.9.3 Total cost of NIHL *69*
5.10 The National Economic Burden Of NIHL 71
5.11 Scenario-Based Sensitivity Analysis 71
    5.11.1 Base case scenario *71*
    5.11.2 Best case scenario *71*
    5.11.3 Worse case scenario *72*

Chapter 6: Discussion 73

    6.1 Introduction 73
    6.2 Proportion Of Potential Workers With NIHL 73
    6.3 Demography Data Of Workers With NIHL 74
    6.4 Hearing Conservation Program In
        Manufacturing Industry 75
        6.4.1 Hearing protection device as noise control *76*
    6.4.2 Attenuation Of Hearing Protection Device 77
        6.4.3 Audiometric Testing Program *78*
    6.5 Input To The Regulatory Impact Analysis (RIA) 80
    6.6 The Average Medical Care Costs 82
    6.7 Considerations On Confounding Factors Of
        NIHL 83
    6.8 Study Strength And Limitations 84

Chapter 7: Conclusion And Recommendations 87

    7.1 Conclusion And Study Findings 87
    7.2 Main Contribution Of This Study 90
    7.3 Recommendation And Future Research 90
    7.4 Overall Conclusions 92

Bibliography 93

LIST OF TABLE

Table 2.1 Non-auditory effects on noise exposure 16
Table 2.2 Occupational diseases in Malaysia 18
Table 2.3 Cost measures and bearer of cost 29
Table 3.1 Study setting 35
Table 3.2 Total number of NIHL cases by region 38
Table 3.3 Scope of questionnaires for workers and employers 39
Table 3.4 Location of data collection for government 40
Table 3.5 Type of data obtained from relevant agencies 40
Table 4.1 Social demography of employer's representatives ... 49
Table 4.2 Percentage of workers exposed to noise 51
Table 4.3 Estimation of workers with NIHL 52
Table 4.4 Incidence rate by industrial classification 53
Table 4.5 Risk of NIHL by industrial classification 54
Table 5.1 Characteristic of workers with NIHL 56
Table 5.2 Workers by industrial classification 57
Table 5.3 Designation and working experience of workers ... 58
Table 5.4 Respondents referred to Medical Centre 59
Table 5.5 Cost of NIHL borne by the workers and employer 61
Table 5.6 Cost of investigation per NIHL case by DOSH ... 67
Table 5.6 Cost of investigation per NIHL case by SOCSO 68
Table 5.7 Total cost of NIHL per worker per year 70
Table 5.8 Scenario based Sensitivity Analysis 72

LIST OF FIGURE

Figure 2.1 Photomicrograph of Cochlea 14
Figure 2.2 Management of Occupational NIHL 21
Figure 2.3 Conceptual Framework of Economic Burden of NIHL among manufacturing workers in Malaysia 33
Figure 4.1 Level of noise exposure 48
Figure 4.2 Implementation of Hearing Conservation Program 50
Figure 4.3 Total workers exposed to noise and total employment 51
Figure 5.1 Symptom of hearing loss among manufacturing workers 58
Figure 5.2 Comparison of direct and indirect expenditures 69

ACKNOWLEDGEMENT

Alhamdulillah, thanks to Allah s.w.t with His permission, we are able to conduct the research and complete this book successfully. We would like to thank Prof. Jamal Hisham Hashim for sharing his knowledge and experience through out the research. An infinite thanks to all the colleagues from the United Nations University International Institute for Global Health (UNU-IIGH) on our true friendship in sharing precious moment to be good researchers.

Noraita Tahir would like to extend her appreciation to the Department of Public Services Malaysia for awarding the *Hadiah Latihan Persekutuan* for her to pursue her postgraduate programme, within which the research that form the basis for this book was undertaken. She also would like to express her great appreciation to her beloved princess, Nada Zafirah Bt Zainal Osman for her patience and understanding during the moment of hardship; her beloved Papa, Hj Tahir B Hj Ahmad and Mak, Hjh. Siti Hawa Bt Hj Mohd Amin, who always pray for her success.

We are indebted to Tan Sri Dato' Dr Mohamed Salleh bin Mohamed Yassin, the Founding Director of UNU-IIGH in providing the international platform of knowledge sharing and the Founding Head of the International Centre for Casemix and Clinical Coding UKM (ITCC-UKM) for providing a conducive research environment to write this book. Our sincere gratitude goes to the Director General of Department of Occupational Safety and Health (DOSH) for giving the trust and confidence for us to carry out the study. We are thankful to the Director of Occupational Health, DOSH and SOCSO who are ever ready to give opinions and support to the success of the study. We would also to thank all health economic lecturers and ITCC-UKM staff who have shared information regarding Casemix in UKM. Our sincere and deepest gratitude goes to all OSH practitioners who are committed in managing the workers who suffer from Noise Induced Hearing Loss (NIHL) during the interviews and the employees who participated in this study.

CHAPTER I
INTRODUCTION

1.1 STUDY BACKGROUND

Noise induced hearing loss (NIHL) is known as one of the most common health issues at the workplace in many countries (Chen & Tsai 2003). The exposures to loud noise damages the hair cells (sensory) in the inner ear permanently and cannot be regenerate and treated (NIDOCD 2008). The number of NIHL cases increases worldwide from 120million (WHO 1999) to 250million in 2004 (Smith 2004). About twenty-two million workers are exposed to potentially damaging noise each year and ten million people in the U.S. have a noise-related hearing loss (NIOSH 2012).

In general, NIHL affected 16% of the workers worldwide (Nelson et al. 2005) in particular that exposed to occupational noise at work. This is the fifteenth most serious health problem in the world (Smith 2004) that attributes to over 4 million DALYs (Disability-Adjusted Life Years) (Nelson et al. 2004). The safe level of noise exposure during work is less than 85 dB (A), however the World Health Organization (1995) estimates approximately 14% of industrial workers worldwide were exposed to noise more than 85 dB (A).

NIHL is an occupational health problem that need to be managed properly especially for developing countries that are rapidly with the development of industrial sectors. At the early phase of industrialization, modern machinery was used in the manufacturing production floor. The machinery emits loud noise exposure to the workers that causing irreversible hearing impairment.

Manufacturing sector has been the common sector for study of NIHL prevalence in Asian countries (Fuente and Hickson 2011). Among high prevalence of NIHL in manufacturing sector in Asian countries were textile industry (Ashraf et. al 2009), (Ni et al. 2007); oil refinery industry (Chen and Tsai 2003); petrochemical plant (Neghab et al. 2009).

In Malaysia, NIHL cases whether occupational or non-occupational supposedly to be manage in accordance to the Guideline of Criteria for the Diagnosis of Occupational Noise Induced Hearing Loss (MOH 2000). Early confirmation on the diagnosis involved noise exposure report from the noise competent person by DOSH. The medical officer whom attended patient or workers with NIHL shall notify Ministry of Health and DOSH by using WEHU E1 & E2 and refer the patient to audiologist for rehabilitation. Evidences collected from audiology and etiology test incurred financial implication to the employers.

NIHL were recorded at 48% of total number of reported occupational diseases and was the highest cases as compared to other diseases since a decade ago (Department of Occupational Safety and Health (DOSH) Malaysia 2011) however, the type of industrial sector affect the workers has not been analyzed. The increasing number of NIHL cases is interpreted as a positive awareness among the employers to comply with the Occupational Safety and Health (Notification of Accident, Dangerous Occurrence, Occupational Poisoning and Occupational Disease) Regulations (2004). It is an obligation for the employer to report any occupational diseases at their place of work under the regulation. Anyhow, reporting to DOSH gives no health benefit to the workers. The employer needs to submit a report to Social Security Organization (SOCSO) and apply for compensation payment and hearing aid facility. In the year 2011, 42% of workers with NIHL were compensated and provided with hearing aid (Social Security Organization Malaysia 2011).

Study on NIHL cases in this country is very much isolated compared to non-communicable disease cases. A study on compliance to hearing conservation program (HCP) were conducted but limited to Negeri Sembilan only (Nor Saleha et al. 2006) and does not describe the prevalence of NIHL at that particular workplaces.

HCP is aimed to protect workers from noise exposure and hence prevent NIHL. The program was introduced in Malaysia under The Factories and Machinery (Noise Exposure) Regulations (1989). Ineffective HCP will give negative effect to reduce noise exposure at work in the manufacturing and mining sectors (WHO 1995).

Compliance to the elements of HCP included policy declaration by the owner and government; noise exposure monitoring; noise control; hearing protection device (HPD); audiometry; education and training and record keeping (Nor Saleha et al. 2006). Although HCP is a mandatory, the method of implementation was not well explained.

Among the HCP's element, noise exposure monitoring and audiometry were the major concern. A competent person registered by DOSH shall conduct both of the elements. The personnel are responsible to measure noise level, conduct audiometric test and prepare a report to the OSH practitioners or person in charge of safety and health at work (Factories and Machinery (Noise Exposure) Regulations 1989). The measurable audiometric effects of occupational NIHL become most noticeable to affected workers in middle age and can be difficult to motivate them to participate in HCP (Dobie 2008).

The industries rely on the efficiency of mobile audiometric services to conduct audiometric test for the workers, some how the ratio between registered silent booth and total industries needed the service were insufficient (DOSH 2011) which impacted in delaying the test results and diagnostics of hearing loss and impairment among workers. Not only that, it will also impressed the annual OSH budget for NIHL management.

Therefore, a comprehensive guideline or code of practice on how to implement effective HCP is urgently needed. The aura of regulatory compliance among the industry players should be transform to the spirit of taking care of workers from hazardous environment.

In the past, health care has not in the attention of economist due to the perception that health care as the right of individuals and the initiatives of the government to provide and organize it. The concept of economic burden of a disease were defined in terms of various measures of economic costs or in terms of various costs borne by different economic agents – government, employer insurers and household/business (Institute of Health Economic 2008). The basic fundamental of total economic burden is the total of direct resource cost, indirect resource cost and losses in health related quality of life. But for the purpose of this research, only the first two elements will be measured. Losses in quality of life are proposed in the further study.

The rising trend of compensation or benefit payment by SOCSO is significant to add value to the burden of the government. The same alternative is a common notion of economic burden that used to measure of the cost burden of diseases in a number of reports (Goeree et al. 1999). A combination of measure of the value of all real resources that are put to NIHL and a measure of lost productivity due to the illness.

By applying The Law of Scarcity, the health care professionals will estimate the sacrifices that implies when a particular service provided with the help of various economic tools. The economic evaluation will benefit the community by showing the right decision of allocating resources despite of influences by the socio-cultural, politic and economic factors.

1.2 RESEARCH QUESTIONS

Being the most significant occupational disease affecting the workforce all over the world, there is uncertainty on the burden of disease in terms of prevalence and financial implication of NIHL in Malaysia. Both of the components are equal important for regulatory impact assessment and estimating the cost benefit of alternative strategies in reviewing the existing noise regulations or drafting a new ones. At present, estimated prevalence of NIHL in manufacturing sectors has been based on evidence from developed countries.

However, study findings from these countries were on very specific industries, sometimes unsuitable to be generalized and replicate for NIHL interventions in Malaysia. Further research is needed to other industrial classifications that will enable to identify more business sectors affected with NIHL by using the same method of this study.

Currently, very limited study findings on investigation of burden of hearing loss due to excessive noise at work. Local studies have focused mainly on contributing factors to hearing loss (Nasir and Rampal 2012); (Noorhassim and Rampal 1998) and hearing conservation program (Nor Saleha 2006). As the reports of NIHL cases were piled up, it signals the greater risks of hearing loss especially machine oriented industries. Hence, estimating safety and health benefits, involving number of workers who will be saved from hearing loss is important, and that it made up the baseline cost of hearing loss caused by the occupational exposure.

In Malaysia, The Factories and Machinery (Noise Regulation) 1989 aimed to protect workers from excessive noise while at work in a limited scope of manufacturing, building construction, mining and quarrying sectors only. Other sectors: Agriculture, Forestry and Fishing, Utilities, Transport and etc. were not covered. The raising trend of NIHL cases were mostly from the manufacturing industries, can be seen as lack of awareness on hazardous risks of noise exposure among the workers and hearing conservation program were not seen as a beneficial investment to the company.

Unfortunately, there is scarcity of data on the financial implication on NIHL in Malaysia to create cost consciousness among the employers and employees. In order to develop a new regulation to cover other place of work, the authority (DOSH) is required to conduct regulatory impact assessment (RIA) that consists of the cost incurred by the employer, employees and the government for each hearing loss cases. RIA is a supportive document to the Attorney General in order to decide in reviewing existing regulations.

Therefore, a cost analysis study is essential for NIHL to quantify the cost borne due to the illness by the society, giving a guide to the policy maker such as Ministry of Human Resources in their budget allocation to maintain Decent Work Agenda (International Labor Organization (ILO)) particularly in prevention of NIHL cases. Principally, this study explores a new perspective of health economics in relation to NIHL. It is strongly believed that NIHL might be a significant occupational disease that is a burden to the country economically.

1.3 RESEARCH SCOPE

The scope of this study will focus on estimating the cost borne by the employer, employee and the government for workers affected with NIHL due to exposure at work in the manufacturing industries. The study will be based on self-reported of occupational disease in Malaysia. The findings of this study will be used as important input to figure out the prevalence and potential NIHL cases for RIA of the existing noise regulations. At the end of the study, the finding of economic burden from the societal perspective will provide financial impact and justification on the development of new regulations for noise exposure.

1.4 RESEARCH JUSTIFICATION

This is a new and unique study that which to our knowledge presently not explored. This study will benefit the government of Malaysia through DOSH to draw a landscape of NIHL cases in by estimating the potential NIHL cases among workers in manufacturing industries that covers 80% of the total industrial sector in Malaysia. The RIA will guide the policy maker to approve the option to review the existing noise regulations (1989) and develop a new regulation with self-regulatory concept. The costing of the NIHL will provide the financial impact of the total expenditure to produce regulatory impact statement.

Despite occupational noise is preventable disease; the situations in developing countries like Malaysia need major improvement specifically in appreciating the occupational noise hazard. Therefore, it is timely important to measure the burden of disease from occupational noise at the national level. Hearing loss is an important outcome impacted from the widespread risk factor of occupational noise. Since the risk is associated with the workplace, therefore the employers as well as the employees were to hold the responsibilities. This assessment will guide the policy maker to inculcate cost-consciousness and further enhance the noise exposure enforcement regime in the country.

Most importantly, the evaluation of costs of NIHL shall assist OSH practitioners including Occupational Health Doctors, ENT Specialist and other related entity in light of the fact to internalize the NIHL from an economic perspective. The expenditures for preventative measures shall be taken as an investment rather than burden to the employers. This study will provide the baseline information and as a template of economic evaluation of occupational diseases in this country as well as to estimate the benefit of prevention of NIHL at work.

1.5 OBJECTIVES OF THE STUDY

A. General

To estimate the cost and economic burden of noise induced hearing loss among workers in Malaysia.

B. Specific

The specific objectives for this research:

a. To estimate the total number of noise induced hearing loss cases among workers in Malaysia;
b. To estimate the total cost borne by:
   i. Employees and their family members for treatment and rehabilitation of NIHL;
   ii. Employers as the payer for treatment and rehabilitation of NIHL;
   iii. Government in managing NIHL;
c. To estimate the Direct Cost and Indirect Cost of NIHL; and
d. To evaluate total economic burden of noise induced hearing loss in Malaysia.

1.6 HYPOTHESIS

The hypothesis of this research:

a. Metal manufacturing industrial workers were the highest risk of NIHL cases in Malaysia.

b. NIHL costs lead to substantial economic burden in this country.
c. The government borne most of the economic burden of NIHL.

CHAPTER II
LITERATURE REVIEW

2.1 INTRODUCTION

This chapter describes the study background in detail based on the literature review reports on NIHL epidemiology; hearing loss outcomes; treatment and rehabilitation; and hearing conservation program. Additional to that, this chapter also reviews the economic cost of NIHL.

2.2 DEFINITION OF NOISE INDUCED HEARING LOSS

Noise induced hearing loss (NIHL) may result from acoustic trauma or chronic exposure to noise over a period of time. It is a sensori-neural hearing loss caused by damage of inner ear that affected hair cells in the cochlear. This is in contrast to occupational acoustic trauma, which is characterized by a sudden change in hearing as a result of a single exposure to a sudden burst of sound, such as an explosive blast. The diagnosis of NIHL is made by the physician, by first taking into account the worker's noise exposure history. Initially, the noise exposure may cause a decrease in hearing sensitivity at a temporary period of time. It may return to its former level within a few minutes to a few hours. The condition can lead to a permanent threshold shift after repeated exposure of excessive noise.

Generally, hearing loss will only be diagnosed if the average hearing loss in both ears were greater than 25 dB in the range from 500 to 3000 Hz (Debra, 1999). NIHL is believed caused by the noise exposure from the working environment but nevertheless non-occupational noise can affect the ear the same as the occupational ones. Non-occupational noise or so-called sociocusis (NIOSH, 1998) includes recreational activities for example listening to loud music or using the fire guns and also household appliances for example using power tools and vacuum cleaner.

2.3 TYPE OF HEARING LOSS

As early as 1956, the effect of noise in the industries was investigated in the St. Vincent Hospital, Dublin (Brian 1956). They observed that young healthy individuals are distressed by intense noise when first exposed it. However, they become accustomed to it after a few days or weeks. They are not aware that noise may be impairing their hearing, because it only involved higher frequency in the early stage, but at a later stage, it will affect the speech frequency.

In general, the possible main causes of hearing loss can be excessive noise (i.e. rock music, construction, gunshot, etc); aging; ear infections; injury to the ear; genetics and ototoxic reaction to drugs. Based on the main causes, hearing loss can be divided into two types: conductive and sensory-neural. But there is still a possibility of a person to get a combination of both types.

Conductive hearing loss caused by the interruptions along the conductive pathway of sound wave to the inner ear, for example excessive ear wax, otitis media (fluid in the middle ear), damaged of ear drum or breakage of tiny bones. All those damages can be corrected by surgery or medication. A synergistic effect on hearing loss was identified under combination exposures to noise and certain physical or chemical agents (e.g., vibration, organic solvents, carbon monoxide, ototoxic drugs and certain metals) (Frank and Morata, 1996). In 1990, Charante and Mulder conducted a study on noise as a contributing factor in industrial accidents but data are insufficient to endorse specific damage risk criteria for these non-audiotory effects (NIOSH, 1998).

In comparison, sensori-nueral hearing loss results from inner ear or auditory nerve dysfunction which caused from heredity/genetics, noise induced hearing loss, head injury, certain medications (damage inner ear hair cells as in Figure 2.1), Illness (measles, mumps, meningitis), normal aging process, birth defects and tumors in the auditory nerve pathway. It is typically irreversible and is a permanent damage to the inner ear. Employees with sensori-nueral hearing loss will experience reduction of sound intensity and lack of clarity in communication.

For the purpose of this study, the researcher will focus on the sensori-nueral type of hearing loss caused by excessive noise exposure.

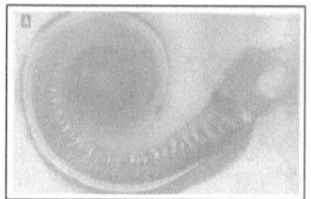 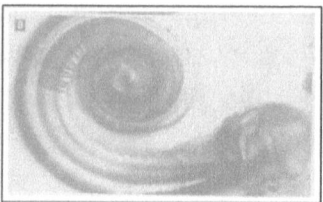

A : Healthy hair cells   B : Damaged hair cells
Figure 2.1 Photomicrograph of Cochlea
Source: Debra 2013

2.4 AUDITORY EFFECTS OF NOISE EXPOSURE

Hearing is a fundamental to communication, which is generally acoustic and oral in nature. It is of great importance to language and socialization. A good quality of life depends on the ability to hear, from communication with family, friends, coworkers, to time of appreciation and time of enjoyment in fact to hearing warning signals. In general, conversation helps people to attune themselves in their social life, chatting over meal, listening to a child or spouse, whisper lovely quotes or playing in the beach.

For industrial workers, good hearing is crucial. It means the ability to identify the deterioration of the machine component or a failure mode and most importantly the ability to detect warning sound for immediate action. Working in the high level of noise environment creates high potential of workplace accidents, have less productive and generate more workplace issues than those working in a lower noise exposure. Messages could be lost or misunderstood and communication can be difficult or impossible even if face-to-face, telephone or using amplified-hearing aid. This condition affects the normal hearing too especially during emergency when evacuation of impaired personals is needed.

Hellen Keller believed to have said that blindness cuts people off from things; deafness cuts people off from people. She is a respected and world-renowned educator who overcame adversity of being blind and deaf. The spouse and family members often feel hearing loss. Spouses have reported that the hearing loss limits companionship and intimate communication. Only most serious matters discussed because more casual conversation can take too much effort (Hetu et al. 1995). Considering the stigma of hearing loss, those with such impairments are subject to stereotyping and prejudice; at times they are presumed to be rude or stupid or both (Noble 1996).

Hearing loss will only be diagnosed if the average hearing loss in both ears were greater than 25 dB in the range from 500 to 3000 Hz from the audiometric test result (Debra 1999). Arithmetic average of the permanent hearing threshold level of an employee at 500, 1000, 2000 and 3000 Hz which is shifted by 25 dB or more compared to the standard audiometric reference level is diagnosed as hearing impairment (Noise regulation 1989). However, standard threshold shift occurred when average shift of more than 10 dB at frequencies of 2000, 3000 and 4000 Hz relative to the baseline audiogram in either ear.

Exposure to excessive noise is a pervasive health hazard which lead to adverse health effects (Table 2.1) including sleeping difficulties, stress, reduced performance, tinnitus, noise induced hearing loss (NIHL) and temporary threshold shift. Among all, the most serious health effect is NIHL, which can results to irreversible damage of the inner ear.

Table 2.1 Non-auditory effects on noise exposure

Physical Effects	Tinnitus
	Increased risk of cardiovascular disease
	Fatigue and sleep deprivation
	Increased accident and injury risk
	Impaired communication
Psychological Effects	Annoyance
	Depression
	Memory Loss
	Impaired decision making
	Difficulty forming and maintaining relationships
	Reduced quality of life
Economic Effects	Employment and income disruption
	Increased employee turnover
	Increased absenteeism
	Reduced productivity and performance

In terms of psychological impacts, workers working in the less noisy environment have less disciplinary action, absenteeism and significantly produce greater productivity. On the other hand, workers who are exposed to noise level of 85 – 95 dBA and wore earmuffs had decreased of cortisol levels and reduced fatigue. Chronic noise exposure increase stress and reduces the quality of life (Noweir 1984). In an earlier study by Weston and Adams (1935) found that 7% to 12% increment in workers personal efficiency while working in the noise level of 96 dBA with hearing protection.

2.5 PREVALENCE OF NIHL

NIHL is a major health problem in Asia due to developing economies in majority of Asian countries that lead to limited access to health services and preventive programs. Fuente (2011) found that prevention of NIHL in Asia were difficult that caused by lack of awareness about NIHL among employers, employees, and health care professionals.

In developing countries like Malaysia, industrialization always linked to the emerging health hazards due to new technologies, materials and operating system implemented. The situation is not always accompanied by protection especially when dealing with occupational noise. A press statement form the Minister of Health in 2008, estimated of 424,000 workers were identified to have hearing problems that were associated with noise exposure at working site (BERNAMA 2008). The figure is rather small as to compare to twenty-two million number of U.S. workers that are exposed to potentially damaging noise each year (NIOSH 2012). Out of that figure, four million workers go to work each day in damaging noise and ten million people in the U.S. have a noise-related hearing loss. In the United States of America (USA), about 30 million workers are exposed to hazardous noise that put them at risk for hearing loss (NIOSH, 2001). In Britain, about 153 000 men and 26 000 women aged 35-64 years were estimated to have severe hearing difficulties attributed to noise at work (Palmer K.T. et al, 2002).

The real time data is unlikely to be made available in Malaysia at the time this thesis was written. There is a lacking of Occupational Health Practitioner in the general hospital that able to relate a disease to the exposure at the workplaces. Since years ago, many researchers conducted studies on the prevalence of hearing loss but very few implement study in estimating number of incidence of NIHL at the workplace. It is recorded that NIHL contributes the highest number of reported cases from the total of incidence rate of occupational diseases in Asia for example in Singapore (2000 - 2009) and the number of NIHL cases recorded reaches more than 86,000 cases in Korea (Fuente 2011).

2.6 INCIDENCE OF NIHL IN MALAYSIA

In 2006, Malaysia rated 2.8 occupational disease incidences per 100,000 workers where the total labor force is 7 million (SOCSO 2010). In the increasing of labor force of Malaysia up to 12.2 million, the number of NIHL reported cases has increased to 1636 cases since year 2003 until 2011 (DOSH 2011). This figure is rather small in compared to the total workforce in this country. No specific data management by the authority that collected occupational disease cases in specific. In most developed countries like Europe a comprehensive documentation of occupational disease were in place but none are completely documented in this country.

In addition, the Department of Occupational Safety and Health (DOSH) are the government agency enforcing the regulation on noise at the workplace recorded an increasing number of reported NIHL cases for the past eight (8) years. NIHL were the highest cases reported compared to other type of diseases (Table 2.2).

Table 2.2 Occupational diseases in Malaysia

Occupational Disease	Year								
	2003	2004	2005	2006	2007	2008	2009	2010	Total
Lungs	13	34	51	38	50	56	57	43	342
Skin	47	79	57	30	192	70	53	78	606
NIHL	**39**	**118**	**190**	**106**	**120**	**169**	**427**	**467**	**1636**
MSD	11	8	22	22	18	31	57	30	187
Biological agent	29	62	139	116	117	41	61	4	569

Source : Department of Occupational Safety and Health 2011

The number of reported cases increases dramatically from 39 in year 2003 to more than 100 cases a year and further increase four times in year 2010, made up a total of 1636 NIHL cases or 48.33% from the total of 3385 occupational diseases/poisoning reported cases in the stretch of eight years.

The analysis on the occupational disease according to industrial sector in 2010 shows even distribution of NIHL reported cases throughout Malaysia but manufacturing sector has the highest case of NIHL with 274 cases out of 467 cases in 2010 (DOSH 2011). This may be due to the usage of machinery at above action level or it might be due to prolong effect of noise that already caused tinnitus to the workers.

In contrast, Social Security Organization (SOCSO) Malaysia reported only 38 invalidity cases and one survivors' case classified under Disorder of the ear and mastoid process in the same year. This figure is rather too small compared to the total of 11,927 and 8,167 numbers of invalidity cases and one survivors' case respectively. The significant difference between cases reported by DOSH and SOCSO is merely due to the function and method of reporting by the employer to the specific agency

2.7 MANAGEMENT OF OCCUPATIONAL NOISE INDUCED HEARING LOSS MANAGEMENT OVERVIEW

Surveillance of Occupational Noise Induced Hearing Loss (NIHL) has been carried out by the National Technical Committee for surveillance of occupational noise induced hearing loss, which is led by the Ministry of Health Malaysia since 1997 (MOH 2000).

The members of the national committee consisted of ENT Specialists, Occupational health Doctors, Audiologists and Engineers from National University of Malaysia (PPUKM), University Malaya, Hospital Kuala Lumpur, Department of Occupational Safety and Health (DOSH), National Institute of Occupational Safety and Health (NIOSH), Social Security Organization (SOCSO) and experts from the ministry.

In the year 2000, the committee published a guideline entitled Criteria for the Diagnosis of Occupational Noise Induced Hearing Loss. This guideline contains definition, diagnosis criteria for NIHL, flowchart for identification and management of occupational NIHL (Figure 2.2) and lastly the guidelines for notification of occupational diseases to the Ministry of Health and DOSH.

The guideline establishes two important evidences; Audiological Evidence and Etiological Evidence in order to confirm the diagnosis of occupational NIHL. The audiological evidence is obtained from the pure tone audiogram performed in the sound proof booth. Whilst, the etiological evidence is retrieved from the measurement of the noise levels at workplace by a competent person registered by DOSH.

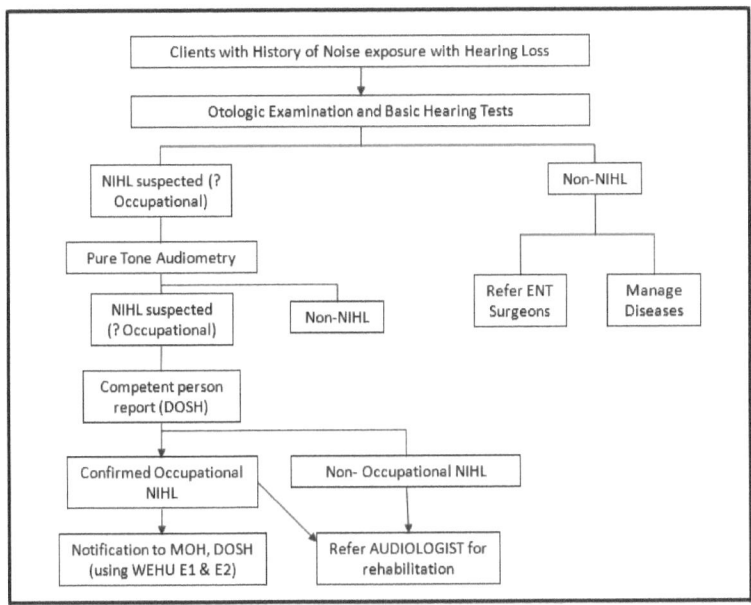

Figure 2.2 Management of Occupational NIHL
Source : MOH 2000

2.8 NOISE EXPOSURE REGULATIONS

The development of Occupational Safety and Health in Malaysia started from the usage of steam boiler at the tin mining industries in 1878, which were in the state of Selangor, Perak, Pahang and Negeri Sembilan (DOSH 2009). The safety enforcement of boilers is referred to Boiler Enactment from each respective state. But none of the enactments cover the heath risk of the inspector or the workers.

In 1882, Holt found "boiler-maker's deafness" upon examined 40 men from the steam boiler workshop in Portland. The effect was clearly identified as loss of hearing. The workers plug their ears with cotton wool and pads but it gave no effect.

In late 1940s, the Hearing Conservation Program began to establish at the aviation and metal industries. Three decades later the Noise Standard promulgated in the United State.

In Malaysia, the aspect of boiler safety is percolated to machinery and workers safety on which the Factories and Machinery Act 1967 (Act 319) were enforced. Specific regulation on noise exposure came into force on 1st of February 1989 namely The Factories and Machinery (Noise Exposure) Regulation 1989. The regulation applied to all factories involving workers exposed to excessive noise level (more than 80 dBA) in the workplace.

In the regulation four clearly stated the responsible of the employer to comply with these regulations. However, in the same regulation there are four responsibilities of the workers such as to co-operate with the employer to wear dosimeter during the noise exposure monitoring; to wear and make full and proper use of hearing protection devices; attend audiometric test and medical examination and attend training provided.

2.8.1 Permissible Exposure Limit (PEL)

Permissible exposure limit is described according to the type of noise level in the Noise Regulations (1989):

i. not exceeding equivalent continuous sound of 90 dBA for eight hours;
ii. not exceeding the limits specified in the First Schedule of Noise Regulations (1989). For example : noise level 85 dBA for 16 hours per day;
iii. not exceeding 115 dBA at any time;
iv. not exceeding a peak sound pressure level of 140 dBA at any time

Initial noise exposure monitoring supposedly to be conducted to determine if any employee may be exposed to noise level at or above the action level of equivalent continuous sound level of 85 dBA. If the result shows that workers are exposed to noise level at or above 85 dBA, positive noise exposure monitoring will be implemented. Both exposure monitoring must be organized by a competent person registered by DOSH and shall use approved noise measuring equipment.

2.8.2 Audiometric program & treatment

Workers whom exposed to noise level at or above 85 dBA are compulsory to attend the audiometric testing program at no cost (Noise Regulation 1989). The test will be conducted by a technician under the supervision of a medical officer registered by DOSH. Audiometric test can only be conducted preceded by a period of at least fourteen hours in a room of pure tone, air conduction, with test frequencies including 500, 1000, 2000, 4000 and 6000 Hz taken separately for each ear. A baseline audiogram and medical history record shall be established within six months from the worker commences work. The test shall be repeated every year for workers exposed to noise level exceeding PEL and those having hearing impairment.

The frequency of audiometric testing depends on the result of the baseline audiogram and condition below (Noise Regulations 1989):

i. Every year if the baseline audiogram shows a hearing impairment or standard threshold shift (average shift of more than 10 dB at frequencies of 2000, 3000 and 4000 Hz);

ii. Every year if workers are exposed to noise level at or above the limits mentioned in 2.8.1;
iii. Once in every two years for workers exposed to noise level at or above 85 dBA but less than the limits described in 2.8.1.

In the occurrence of STS, the medical practitioners were responsible to notify DOSH officer and inform the workers with the test result. The workers shall be provided with hearing protection device (HPD) including refit and retrain in the use of HPD. Nor Saleha (2006) found 1926 employees among industries in Negeri Sembilan who were exposed to noise had undergone audiometric test and only 5.2% of them had standard threshold shift (STS).

2.8.3 Control measures

Two main methods of control measure for noise exposure are engineering control and administrative control. Engineering control involves installation of a certain control measures at the source of noise as far as reasonably practical to the working area, whilst administrative control monitored the workers noise exposure for example by job rotation. When either of the above methods are not sufficient, the workers were supplement with hearing protection devices. It is responsibility of employers to provide workers with approved type of hearing protection devices (HPD) at no cost. HPD is mandatory for workers who are expose to noise level at or above PEL. It must correctly fit the worker, compatible with the job requirement and does not give health effect to the workers.

The main function of HPD is to attenuate the noise exposure to below action level (85 dBA). Hence, a complete procedure on the issuance, maintenance, inspection and training in the use of HPD must be implemented for effective hearing protection. A study among forging plants workers in Northern India found that majority of them were not wearing HPD suffer from NIHL (Singh et al. 2009). Every affected worker shall be given a training that comprises of provision of noise regulations; effects of noise on hearing; about the HPD – advantages, disadvantages; attenuations of various type of hearing protection; instructions on their selection; fitting, use and care; and purpose of audiometric testing.

2.8.4 Warning Signs and record keeping

Warning signs are normally posted at the entrances to working area with noise exposure above PEL. It must indicate the high noise area signage and an icon of HPD to emphasis that all entries must protect their hearing. The employers shall keep good records records regarding exposure monitoring and audiometric test were to be maintained as long as the workers is employed and thereafter for five years.

2.9 HEARING HEALTHCARE PROFESSIONALS

Before a person can be prescribed with hearing loss, he will need to be referred to hearing loss professionals namely audiologists, hearing aid specialists and otolaryngologists functions at different levels of hearing treatment. Audiologists identify and assess disorders of the hearing and dispense amplification system for the employee such as hearing aids and related devices; program cochlear implant; provide instruction;

rehabilitation and counseling services. Hearing aid specialists assess hearing and select, fit and dispense hearing aid and related devices. They provide instruction, rehabilitation and counseling in the use, care of hearing aids. Otolaryngologists are ear, nose and throat physicians whom perform a complete medical history and physical examination of the head and neck. They also supervise hearing and balance testing which lead to medical diagnosis and treatment that include prescribing medications; performing surgery; implanting cochlear implants; selecting, fitting and dispensing hearing aids.

2.10 POSSIBLE TREATMENT FOR HEARING LOSS

As far as the researcher's review, there is yet a specific medical care treatment for hearing loss due to noise exposure. However the most popular option is rehabilitation by using hearing aids and the Cochlear Implant System for severe sensori-neural hearing loss cases. The second option is rather costly. The U.S. National Council in the Aging (1999), found that hearing loss is commonly related to aging population. Survey on more than 2000 people with hearing loss showed that treatment can improve earning power, intimacy and warmth family relationship, emotional stability, sense of control over life events and also perception of mental functioning.

2.11 HEARING CONSERVATION PROGRAMME AND REQUIREMENTS OF THE LAW

A precious gift by God to his man; the ability to hear and the ability to experience to hear a range of sound that are full, boisterous, tender, clean and pure that adds beauty to life. Hearing conservation required personal motivation and perseverance of individual action in both occupational and non-occupational settings (Berger, 2000). Implementing Hearing Conservation Program (HCP) in the workplace can be meaningful and effective in the prevention of hearing loss. With having this program, it deliver add-on value to the return of investment in terms of benefits related to the employees; enhanced attitudes, improved productivity and better image. The World Health Organization reported an increasing of excessive noise exposure in developing countries in the informal expert consultation in 1997. High noise exposure levels in African region occurred in manufacturing and mining sectors are due to the absence of effective prevention program for NIHL.

WHO remarked that between one-fifth and one-third of workers have NIHL in most South-East Asia countries the situation is different. Most countries might already have NIHL prevention program and legislations. However, the implementation and enforcement is mostly poor.

In developed country like Japan, shipbuilding industry was found to have the highest cases of NIHL and most compensation has been paid. Noise control and hearing conservation program conducted includes audiometric test during recruitment and relocation every six months, education and training to workers as well as supervisors.

2.12 STUDY ON COSTS OF HEARING LOSS

Study of economic is a study of how men and society choose with or without the use of money to employ scarce productive resources to produce goods and services over time and distribute them for consumption, now and in the future among various people and groups in society (Institute of Health Economics 2008). But in the past, health care has not in the attention of economist due to the perception that health care as the right of individuals and the initiatives of the government to provide and organize it.

Later in the 19th century, the cost of health care increase, consumer changed their attitude and demand pattern and the government seems unable to provide appropriate level of health care to its citizen. Many factors cause health care to being considered as commodity and economist think that it might contribute to solve health care problems. The law of scarcity helps the health economist to estimate the implication of a service provider by various economic tools.

The concept of economic evaluation of a disease could be defined in terms of various measures of economic costs or in terms of various costs borne by different economic agents – government, employer insurers and household/business. The basic tasks of any economic evaluation in healthcare would be to identify, measure, value and compare costs and consequences of alternative programs being considered (Drummond et al. 2005).

The general rule when assessing programs is that difference in costs is compared with the difference in consequences in an incremental analysis. The cost measures were classified as direct and indirect resource costs, transfer or insurance payment or disability benefit and health status based on losses in health quality of life as illustrated in Table 2.3.

The decision on the cost analysis study depends on the analysis point of view, whether it includes the society, government in general, the patient or the worker and/or the employer (Drummond et al. 2005). In general, the health economic evaluation is a comparative analysis of alternative courses of action in terms of costs and health consequences.

The ultimate goal for the measurement is to allocate resource scarcity faced by an organization or the society in general.

Table 2.3 Cost measures and bearer of cost

Cost measure		Bearer of Cost		
		Government	Private Insurers	Households/ Business

Resource costs	Direct health and social care resources	• Health Ministry
		• Other Ministries
		   - Housing
		   - Education
		   - Social services
		   - Non-insured services for the handicapped
			Non-insured health services (e.g. pharmaceuticals)	Goods and services paid out of pocket (e.g. pharmaceuticals)

	Indirect resources (lost productivity)	Not relevant	Not relevant	• Presenteeism • Absenteeism • Short term work loss • Work loss due to premature mortality • Caregiver time
Transfers	Transfer (non-resources payment)	• Assured income for the severely handicapped • Disability benefit • Employment insurance	Insurance disability payment	
Losses in Health related Quality of Life	Health Status	Not relevant	Not relevant	Lost Quality Adjusted Life Years (QALY's)

Source : Institute of Health Economics (2008)

For the purpose of this master thesis, the researcher will measure resource costs that include the direct and indirect health resources from the perspective government and household/business. The researcher will separate the household/business into two different bearers; the workers and the employers. The World Health Organization (WHO) categorized the resource costs as direct, indirect and intangible cost. The cost of illness constitutes the resources that are spent on treatment, control and prevention of malaria by households, health institutions, the government and her development partners (Goeree et. al 1999; Asante et. al 2003).

2.12.1 Direct cost

Direct cost refers to resources use that are traced and attributed to the intervention or treatment regime. It specifically associated with a particular unit or department or employee (Judith and Baker 2006). Direct costs or Direct Resources Cost is the costs of illness and social care services by providers or agencies related. For example cost by the government include hospital services, general practitioners, pharmaceuticals, and etc. Cost by the employer includes the pharmaceuticals and hearing device and cost by the employee is the out of pocket to pay the bills. A combo costs comprises of personal, household, institutional and government expenditures on both prevention and treatment as the direct cost (Asante 2010).

However, top down costing approach suitable to estimate the direct cost of in-patient and outpatient treatment (Aljunid et al. 2010). The approach enables the researcher to estimate cost per day stay per case for in-patient cases. Outpatient treatment costs is estimated as annual outpatient resource use to be multiplied by unit treatment charges by the hospital.

2.12.2 Indirect cost

In comparison, indirect cost refers to resources that are allocated or assigned o a particular object. In economic point of view, indirect cost is referred to productivity loss related to illness (Shahram 2001). The cost, which is also labeled as Indirect Resource Cost, is related to cost of work loss or productivity loss resulting from partial and long term disability. This type of costs can be measured by estimating the insurance payment or compensation in employment income. The societal analysis is used to estimate loss of productivity by multiplying the number of leave days by the average gross domestic product per capita per day (Aljunid et al. 2010).

2.12.3 Economic burden

The total burden of NIHL from the societal perspective is the total of direct and indirect average costs per employee by the prevalence number of cases. However, the total burden of illness from the provider's perspective is suggested to include direct medical costs (Aljunid et al. 2010).

The cost analysis is a partial economic evaluation. Usually the outcome will not be the focus of the evaluation but the important subject is to identify the important cost involved. This is due to the difficultness to measure and value all costs or all alternatives costs. The total cost of disease can be the hint in the scenario-based sensitivity analysis.

2.13 RESEARCH CONCEPTUAL FRAMEWORK

The research focused on the economic burden measurement on the direct and indirect costs Occupational Noise Induced

Hearing Loss (NIHL) borne by the three party; the workers affected with NIHL due to exposure to noisy working environment and the caregiver; the employer and the government.

The first part of the measurement involved the workers with NIHL, whom were refer to the medical care centre for treatment and rehabilitation. At the same time, the usage of alternative treatment were also included in the survey. The workers were needed attend awareness/skill training provided by the employer every year based on the requirement of the Noise regulation. Hence, the direct cost borne by the workers/caregiver for medical care, non-medical care and transportation were measured and the indirect cost were measure from the loss of time atteding medical care and training.

The second part involved the employer, the based on the medical care cost, on site audiometric testing and transportation provided for workers' medical care trip and loss of productive time due to attending medical care. Loss of productive years were also checked among the employers that have workers affected with NIHL. The direct cost for the employer were measured from the medical care cost and transportation and the indirect cost involved productivity loss attending medical care, testing and training.

The last part of the study were to measure the burden of the government agencies involved with the case. In this part, the researcher measured the medical care cost based on top down costing from previous study. While the investigation of occupational NIHL were carried out by Department of Occupaional Safety and Health (DOSH) and Social Security Organization (SOCSO) officers for each cases. Further to that, SOCSO provide benefit payment to the affected workers. The direct cost for the government were measured from the medical cost while the indirect cost measured were investigation cost and benefit expenditure. In this framework (Figure 2.2), all measured cost were coded by the colour; workers (blue), caregiver (pink), employer (yellow) and government (green). Boxes with combination of color means that the costs is shared between the three party.

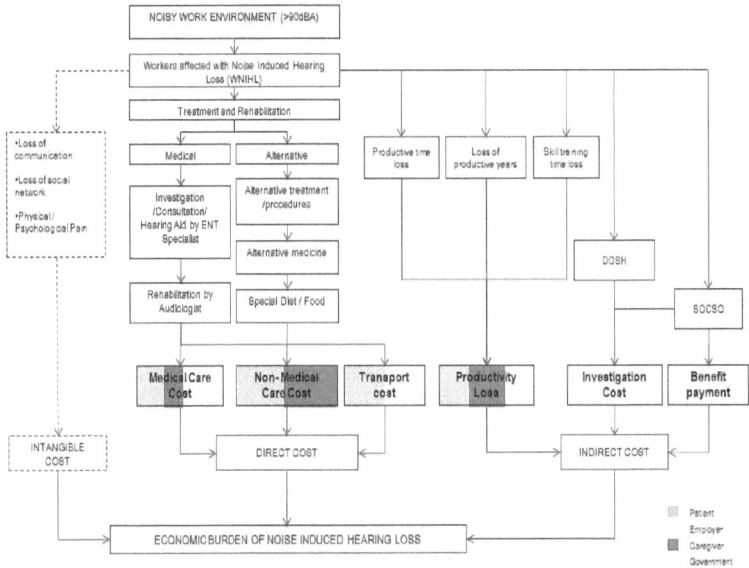

Figure 2.3 Conceptual Framework of Economic Burden of NIHL among manufacturing workers in Malaysia

CHAPTER III
RESEARCH METHODOLOGY

3.1 INTRODUCTION

This chapter covered the methodology used and the flow of approaches of the study to achieve the research objectives. In short, the study were conducted at the manufacturing industries with NIHL cases, to identify the type of industries potentially high in NIHL cases and using the economic evaluation to estimate the cost of NIHL to furnish the regulatory impact assessment to justify new set of noise regulation.

3.2 STUDY DESIGN

This is a descriptive cross sectional study at manufacturing industries with highest reported NIHL cases to DOSH in Malaysia in year 2011. The workers and the employer were asked to state the amount of money they spend for NIHL treatment and rehabilitation including transport and productivity time loss in the pass one year. Data on noise exposure level were collected from the employer in each industry.

3.3 STUDY SETTING AND STUDY DURATION

The study was carried out at the manufacturing industries in 12 group of industrial classification that operates in five states. Each region comprises states in Peninsular Malaysia; Pulau Pinang (North), Selangor (Central), Johor (South), Terengganu and Kelantan (East). The survey was carried out started from November 2012 to November 2014.

Table 3.1 Study setting

Industrial Classification/Region	North	South	Central	East
Food	1	1	1	2
Tobacco	0	0	1	0
Textile	2	0	0	0
Wearing Apparel	1	0	0	0
Wood	1	0	0	0
Paper	0	0	1	1
Refined Petroleum	0	0	0	2
Chemicals	0	0	2	1
Non-metallic product	0	1	0	0
Metal	2	1	0	2
Fabricated metal	1	0	1	0
Motor vehicle & component	0	1	0	0
Total	8	4	6	8

3.4 SAMPLING FRAME

The population in this survey was workers whom are working in the manufacturing industries with noise level more than 90 dBA. A total of 517 potential participants were identified from the database of NIHL cases reported to DOSH in 2011. The sample of employers and location of industries was selected from the manufacturing industries reported to DOSH with highest number of NIHL cases in the same year.

3.5 INCLUSION AND EXCLUSION CRITERIA

The inclusion and exclusion criteria were used to screen the participant for the survey, as listed below:

a. Inclusion Criteria
   i. Working in the manufacturing industries with noise exposure level at or more than action level (85 dBA);
   ii. Manufacturing industries of food, tobacco, textile, wearing apparel, wood products except furniture, paper, refined petroleum, chemicals, non-metallic mineral, basic metal, fabricated metal, motor vehicle parts; and
   iii. NIHL cases reported to DOSH by using Form JKKP 7.

b. Exclusion Criteria
   i. Workers with conductive hearing loss;
   ii. Workers affected with ear infections and diseases;
   iii. Manufacturing industries located in Sabah, Sarawak and Labuan; and
   iv. Manufacturing industries other than a.ii.

3.6 SAMPLE SIZE

The sample size was determined from Kretcjie and Morgan (1970) guidelines for planning a survey.

$$S = \frac{X^2 NP(1-P)}{d^2(N-1) + X^2 P(1-P)}$$

where
- S = required sample size
- N = the population size = 517
- P = population proportion (0.5 yields the maximum possible sample size)
- d = 0.05, the degree of accuracy as reflected by the amount of error that can be tolerated in the fluctuation of a sample population proportion P
- X^2 = 3.841 (based on 0.95 confidence level)

Hence,

$$S = \frac{3.841(517)(0.5)(1-0.5)}{(0.05)^2(517-1) + 3.841(0.5)(1-0.5)}$$

$$= 221 \text{ samples.}$$

Allowing for 5% margin of error, with 95% confidence interval and population proportion of 0.5 based on the assumption that almost half of the workers exposed to noise level at or more than 90 dBA diagnosed with NIHL. The calculated size of sample required for the survey was 221 samples. However, the researcher will take all 372 workers reported with NIHL based on the location of study settings in Peninsular Malaysia as in Table 3.2.

Table 3.2 Total number of NIHL cases by region

Region	Total NIHL cases
Northern (Pulau Pinang)	162
Southern (Johor)	30
Central (Selangor)	113
East (Pahang & Terengganu)	67
Total	372

3.7 DATA COLLECTION TOOLS

The study will be conducted in a mix method by using questionnaires and in-depth interview. Two types of questionnaires were administered to the workers (QP) and employer (QE) respectively as the data collection tool as in Appendix A and B. Questionnaires were distributed during the face-to-face interview with the workers. The occupational health division officer from local DOSH office accompanied the researcher at the respective states.

A cover letter from the Deputy Director General of DOSH Malaysia is send to the factory manager or OSH practitioner of relevant industries upon receiving approval from the Ethiques Committee. Incomplete questionnaires during the interview will be provided with self-addressed envelope and stamps to be return to the researcher. Both questionnaires, QP and QE were divided into six (6) parts as in Table 3.3:

Table 3.3 Scope of questionnaires for workers and employers

	Questionnaires for Worker (QP)	Questionnaires for Employer (QE)
Part 1	Background	Background
Part 2	General Information about current job	General Information about employer's representative
Part 3	Medical Care and Alternative Care for Hearing Loss	Noise exposure management
Part 4	Transportation for Treatment and Rehabilitation	Treatment and Rehabilitation of NIHL
Part 5	Caregiver for the worker	Transportation
Part 6	Productive Years Loss	Productivity Loss

A validity test on both questionnaires QP and QE were carried out to 10 workers with NIHL and the OSH practitioner of an industry in Kulim, Kedah to review the understanding of respondent to respond to the questionnaires. Improvements of the existing questionnaires were done based on the responds of both parties and the respond time.

An information sheet in Appendix C were prepared and distributed with a consent statement form to all workers whom involved in this study. The information sheet contains of title of research, introduction, objectives, involvement, the benefits, the risks, and confidentiality, taking part, withdrawal, payment and contacts. Upon reading and understanding the information sheet, the workers put down their signature in the consent form as in Appendix D.

3.8 DATA COLLECTION FOR GOVERNMENT

The data of medical expenses for treatment and rehabilitation of NIHL by the government medical centre were collected from the top down costing for outpatient conducted by the

International Centre for Casemix and Clinical Coding, UKM Medical Centre Kuala Lumpur. However, the expenditure on the investigation of NIHL cases and total benefit paid to the workers were calculated from data collected from DOSH and SOCSO. Data were collected through face-to-face interviews of the officers in each agency as listed in Table 3.4 and type of data obtained as in Table 3.5:

Table 3.4 Location of data collection for government

Agency	Location
Government Medical Centre	International Centre for Casemix and Clinical Coding, UKM Medical Centre
DOSH	• Occupational Health Division, DOSH Putrajaya • Occupational Health Section, DOSH Selangor
SOCSO	• Occupational Health Division, SOCSO K.Lumpur • SOCSO Kajang Branch office

Table 3.5 Type of data obtained from relevant agencies

Agency	Officer	Data obtained
DOSH	• Director of Occupational Health Division, DOSH headquarters, Putrajaya • Occupational Health Nurse from each region	▪ Procedure of NIHL investigation; ▪ Duration time spend for NIHL investigation; ▪ Number of officers involved; ▪ Amount of salary;
SOCSO	• Manager of SOCSO Kajang Selangor	• Procedure of investigation on NIHL; • Frequency of visit for investigation; • Duration time spend for the investigation; • Number of officers involved • Amount of salary
	• Medical officer of SOCSO headquarters, Kuala Lumpur	• Medical Board Decision • Total benefit payment

3.9 DATA ANALYSIS

A mixed method analysis was conducted for the data collected. Quantitative data were analyzed by using MS-Excel and Statistical Package for Social Sciences ® (IBM-SPSS) version 20.0.

3.9.1 Estimation of total number of NIHL cases among manufacturing workers

Based on a list of manufacturing industries that reported the highest NIHL cases obtained (DOSH 2011), industries were classified according to Malaysia Standard Industrial Classification (2008). The researcher assumes that the industries listed are highly potential to affect workers with NIHL in long term. Estimation on the potential workers with NIHL is calculated by multiplying the percentage of workers exposed to noise more than 85 dBA and the total employment based on economic censors (2011).

Equation 1:

$$\text{Percentage of the workers exposed to noise} = \frac{\text{Total number of workers with NIHL}}{\text{Total employment in the industry}}$$

Equation 2:

$$\text{Potential workers with NIHL} = \text{Percentage of the workers exposed to noise} \times \text{Total employment based on Economic Census}$$

Equation 3:

$$\text{Incidence rate of NIHL} = \frac{\text{Total NIHL case reported}}{\text{Total employment on Economic Census}}$$

3.9.2 Total cost of NIHL

A database format will be created as an input data tool to analyze the cost borne by the employer, workers, caregiver and the government. A calculation template was based on previous relevant studies on economic burden (Aljunid et. al 2010; Judith and Baker 2006). The cost of each cost component was taken in average of one worker with NIHL per year. A costing template based on annual average cost for each worker with NIHL is designed taking consideration of direct and indirect cost.

Based on the conceptual framework, the direct cost of NIHL (C_{direct}) includes medical care, rehabilitation, on-site audiometric and transportation. Medical care cost includes payment for every treatment, rehabilitation, pharmacy, medical leave and medical equipment. Medical care cost is labeled as C_M and the on-site audiometric test compliance cost is labeled as C_{AT}. The cost of transportation (C_T) or fuel fees was considered as journey from worker's house or factory to the medical centre and return, besides company transportation.

For the indirect cost of NIHL ($C_{indirect}$) involves loss of productive time (C_p) in which when workers spend their time out from working activities such as medical care, on-site audiometric test, awareness training and over time and absenteeism. Despite having hearing loss, the workers still need to attend annual awareness training; hence, the cost of training is labelled as C_{Tg}.

At the perspective of law enforcement, investigation will be conducted for NIHL cases reported to the relevant authority for improvement and procedures of benefit payment. Both of the costs are labeled as C_{Inv} and C_{Ben} respectively. In the case of alternative care, the costs were included prescription of alternative treatment, procedures and herbal medication and labeled as C_A.

This study will gather information and data of the total expenditure to the worker (W), employers (E) and the government (G) on the costs of NIHL that relevant to them. Detail of costs calculated for each party was discussed in the chapter below.

3.9.2.1 Estimating the cost of NIHL by workers and caregivers

The cost of NIHL by the workers and caregiver were estimated from expenses on medical care, alternative care and transportation as Equation 4 and 5:

Equation 4 :
Cost borne by worker, $C_W = (C_M + C_A + C_T)_W$

Equation 5:
Cost borne by caregiver, $C_C = (C_M + C_A + C_T + C_P)_C$

3.9.2.2 Estimating the cost of NIHL by employers

The expenditure for NIHL cases to the employer considered in this study was cost for medical care, transportation and loss of production time as in Equation 6.

Equation 6:
Cost borne by employer, $C_E = (C_M + C_T + C_P)_E$

Where :
The cost for loss of productive time for workers, caregiver or employer were calculated as below

$$C_P = \frac{\text{Salary per month}}{8 \text{ working hours} \times 24 \text{ days}} \times \text{Time spend for medical care}$$

3.6.2.3 Estimating cost of NIHL by government

The cost of NIHL to the government consisted hospital medical expenditure for treatment and rehabilitation of NIHL; Investigation cost by occupational health officers from DOSH and investigation and benefit expenditure by SOCSO as Equation 7.

Equation 7 :

Cost borne by government, $C_G = (C_M + C_{Inv} + C_{Ben})_G$

Where :
- C_M = Cost of treatment for outpatient from top down costing at surgery clinic UKMMC
- C_{Inv} = (Time taken per task per case X Salary per hour) for DOSH & SOCSO Officers
- C_{Ben} = $\frac{\text{Total expenditure (Permanent Disability \& Temporary Disability)}}{\text{No. of case per year in 2011}}$

3.9.2.4 Estimating the Direct Cost of NIHL

The direct cost of NIHL cause spending on the medical cares cost, alternative care and transportation by worker, caregiver, employer and the government accordingly as Equation 8.

Equation 8:

Direct Cost of NIHL, $C_{direct} = C_{M(W+C+E+G)} + C_{A(W+C)} + C_{T(W+C+E)}$

3.9.2.5 Estimating the Indirect Cost of NIHL

The indirect cost of NIHL contains all costs for productive time loss, awareness training, investigation of NIHL by DOSH/SOCSO and also total benefit paid to the affected workers by SOCSO as Equation 9.

Equation 9:

Indirect Cost of NIHL, $C_{indirect} = C_{P(W+C+E)} + C_{Tg} + C_{Inv} + C_{Ben}$

3.9.2.6 Estimating the Total Cost of NIHL

The total cost of NIHL is the summation direct cost and indirect cost of NIHL that also considered as the national economic burden of NIHL per worker per year.

Equation 10:

Total economic burden of NIHL, $C_{NIHL} = (C_{direct} + C_{indirect})$

W, C, E, G

CHAPTER IV

RESULTS: ESTIMATION OF NIHL CASES AMONG MANUFACTURING WORKERS

4.1 INTRODUCTION

This chapter reports the results from of the estimation on NIHL cases among the manufacturing workers. Type of manufacturing industries involved in this study was listed in this chapter and details of research methodology were in Chapter 3.

4.2 PROFILES OF MANUFACTURING INDUSTRIES HAVING WORKERS WITH NIHL

Based on the list of NIHL cases (DOSH 2011), 26 industries in manufacturing sectors were identified and have been classified by MSIC (2008) as in Table 9. Questionnaires were distributed to OSH practitioner that represent the employer of each industry. The main purpose of distributing the questionnaires were to gather data on the total number of workers exposed to noise more than action level and implementation of hearing conservation program. Respondents of the study were Safety and Health Practitioners, Plant Managers, EHS Managers/Executives and HR Officers. For this particular chapter they were called employers. The response rate from the employer is 100%.

4.3 DEMOGRAPHIC DATA OF EMPLOYERS

A total of 26 OSH practitioners represent the employer of 26 manufacturing industries for in-depth interviews guided with questionnaires. They have working experience ranging from 1 to 31 years in occupational safety and health were involved in this study. They were predominantly male (85%) and Malays (81%). More than half (58%) of the employer's representatives hold managerial positions in their industries respectively. Table 10 shows the social demographic data of employer's representatives who took part in this study.

4.4 NOISE LEVEL EXPOSURE IN THE INDUSTRIES

The level of noise exposure collected from the study sites was divided into two (2) categories as in Figure 4.1. Almost 70% of the manufacturing industries were exposed to noise level more than action level of 85 dBA (86-90 dBA) namely tobacco, textile, wearing apparel, paper, refined petroleum, sheet glass and fabricated metal factories. The noise exposure level in the wooden pallet and automotive filter factories were found more than permissible exposure limit of 90 dBA (91-140 dBA). From the database of DOSH (2011), the researcher found that both level of noise exposure contributed high NIHL cases among the workers in the manufacturing industries.

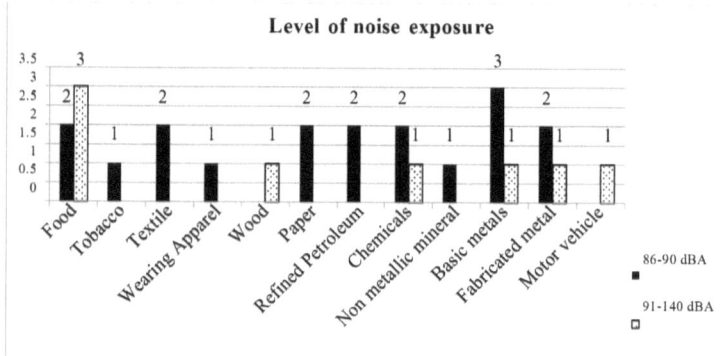

Figure 4.1 Level of noise exposure

The data showed that although industries were classified under food industry, but the palm oil processing plants (3) had higher noise level as compared to the chocolate (1) and animal feed (1) industry. In chemical industries, pesticides (1) and industrial gas (1) factories exposed to lower range noise level compared to engineering plastic factories. Where as in basic metal industries, manufacturer of magnetic wire and steel bar (1) were identified having higher range noise level, in contrary to the steel bar (3) manufacturers.

Table 4.1 Social demography of employer's representatives

Social demography data	Frequency (n=26)	Percentage (%)
Gender		
Male	22	85
Female	4	15
Race		
Malay	21	81
Chinese	5	19
Designation		
Manager	15	58
Executive	4	15
Officer	6	23
Nurse	1	4
Years of employment (years)		
1 – 4	10	38
5 - 9	4	15
10 – 14	5	19
15 - 20	2	8
> 20	5	19

4.5 IMPLEMENTATION OF HEARING CONSERVATION PROGRAM

In this matter, employer's representatives were asked on the implementation of hearing conservation program in the workplace as in Figure 4.2. All responded industries conducted regular awareness training on noise exposure and hearing protection to the workers. Hearing protection device (HPD) were distributed to all workers exposed to noise. About half of respondents provided earplug and the other half provided both earplug and earmuff for their workers.

HPD utilizes by all responded industries attenuate the employee exposure to noise level below PEL or action level. Unfortunately, none of the industries validate the attenuation of HPD fitted at each worker.

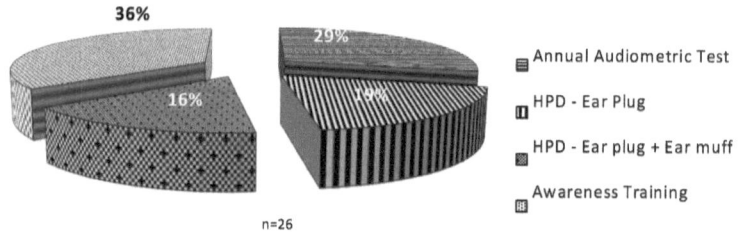

Figure 4.2 Implementation of Hearing Conservation Program

4.6 ESTIMATION OF THE TOTAL NUMBER OF NIHL CASES AMONG MANUFACTURING WORKERS

Based on the data from the employer, a total of 4,612 workers identified were exposed to noise more than action level (86 – 140 dBA) at 8 hours per day continuously in a year with total employment of 11,457 workers in 26 industries as in Figure 4.3. Percentage of workers exposed to noise was then calculated from the two data obtained and resulted as in Table 4.2.

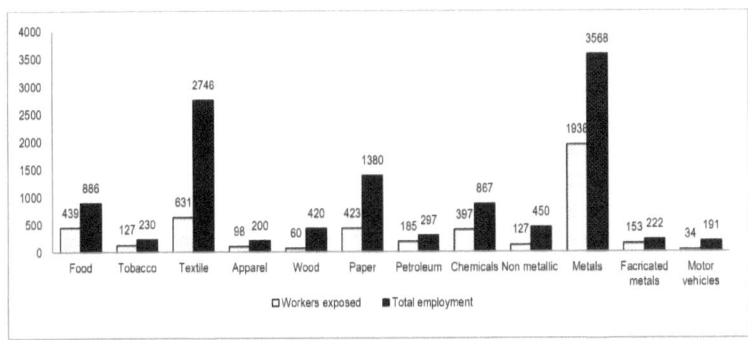

Figure 4.3 Total workers exposed to noise and total employment

Table 4.2 Percentage of workers exposed to noise

Industrial Classifications	Total no of. Workers exposed to noise	Total employment	Percentage of workers exposed to noise
Food	439	886	49.5%
Tobacco	127	230	55.2%
Textile	416	741	56.1%
Wearing Apparel	320	2352	13.6%
Wood	98	200	49.0%
Paper	268	800	33.5%
Refined Petroleum	358	1240	28.9%
Chemicals	334	577	57.9%
Non metallic mineral	127	450	28.2%
Basic metals	1938	3568	54.3%
Fabricated metal	153	222	68.9%
Motor vehicle	34	191	17.8%
Total	4612	11457	

Further analysis was conducted to estimate the total number of workers potential with NIHL based on the total population of manufacturing workers in the Economic Census Report in 2011 at the manufacturing industries classified according to MSIC 2008. The percentage of workers exposed to noise level more than action level is about 40.3% and the total potential workers affected with NIHL were estimated to be 103,673 workers as in Table 4.3.

Table 4.3 Estimation of workers with NIHL

Industrial Classifications*	Total employment**	Percentage of workers exposed to noise***	Estimated workers with NIHL
Food	51466	49.5%	25501
Tobacco	2543	55.2%	1404
Textile	11666	56.1%	6549
Wearing Apparel	40022	13.6%	5445
Wood	3330	49.0%	1632
Paper	28725	33.5%	9623
Refined Petroleum	6915	28.9%	1996
Chemicals	30445	57.9%	17623
Non metallic mineral	9332	28.2%	2634
Basic metals	33453	54.3%	18170
Fabricated metal	8182	68.9%	5639
Motor vehicle	41885	17.8%	7456
Total	**267964**	**40.3%**	**103673**

Note :
* Industries were classified from Malaysia Standard Industrial Classification, 2008.
** Based on Economic Census 2011
*** Noise level more than 85 dBA at a prolonged exposure continuously in a year.

4.7 INCIDENCE RATE AND RISK OF NIHL CASES AMONG MANUFACTURING WORKERS

The incidence rate was estimated from the total NIHL cases and total population of manufacturing workers. Tobacco industries marked the highest incidence of NIHL (1140 per 100,000 workers) among all industries. High noise level might be produced from the cigarette-packing machine in the factory. This was followed by refined petroleum (434 per 100,000 workers) and textile (343 per 100,000 workers) incidence. In overall, total employment of all manufacturing industries were 267,964 workers and resulted 139 incidence of NIHL in every 100,000 workers. Detail of the incidence rate as in Table 4.4.

Table 4.4 Incidence rate by industrial classification

Industrial Classification	Total NIHL case*	Total employment **	Incidence per 100,000 workers
	(a)	(b)	((a/b) x 100,000)
Food	30	51466	58
Tobacco	29	2543	1140
Textile	40	11666	343
Wearing Apparel	32	40022	80
Wood	6	3330	180
Paper	36	28725	125
Refined Petroleum	30	6915	434
Chemicals	41	30445	135
Non metallic mineral	6	9332	64
Basic metals	89	33453	266
Fabricated metal	22	8182	269
Motor vehicle	11	41885	26
Total	**372**	**267964**	**139**

Note :
* Real time NIHL cases reported in 2011
**Total employment from Economic Census 2011

The highest risk of NIHL determined in Table 4.5 is motor vehicle industries. The industry involved manufacturing of oil filter casing using metal plate. Even though the industrial classification by MSIC (2008) separated basic metal, fabricated metal and motor vehicle but the industries were still handling with metal. Hence, the hypothesis made by the researcher is proven that metal industry is at the highest risk.

Table 4.5 Risk of NIHL by industrial classification

Industrial Classification	Total NIHL cases	Total workers exposed >AL	Risk (%)
	c	d	(c/d) X 100
Food	30	439	7%
Tobacco	29	127	23%
Textile	40	416	10%
Wearing Apparel	32	320	10%
Wood	6	98	6%
Paper	36	268	13%
Refined Petroleum	30	358	8%
Chemicals	41	334	12%
Non metallic mineral	6	127	5%
Basic metals	89	1994	4%
Fabricated metal	22	97	23%
Motor vehicle	11	34	32%

CHAPTER V

RESULTS: COST AND ECONOMIC BURDEN OF NIHL IN MANUFACTURING INDUSTRIES IN MALAYSIA

5.1 INTRODUCTION

This chapter reports the results from of the estimation the economic burden of NIHL cases in manufacturing industries in Malaysia. The research methodology of sampling and data collection were discussed in Chapter 3.

5.2 PROFILES OF MANUFACTURING WORKERS WITH NIHL

The initial target of the survey was to all 372 workers reported with NIHL cases in Peninsular Malaysia. However, only 310 workers reported with NIHL attended as the respondents in the face-to-face interview and fill up the questionnaires. The number of respondent present is sufficient as to compare with the sampling size of 221 respondents.

Among the workers with NIHL, 91% (283) of them were male and 9% (27) were female workers aged between 24 to 60 years old. 283 (93%) of respondents were married and only 27 of them are still single. A significant percentage of respondent were Malay (71%), followed by 13% of Chinese, 13% of India 3% of other races including Indonesian, Bangladeshi, Vietnamese and Nepalese (3%). Majority of workers attained secondary education (79%), while 11% and 10% were at primary and university level of education respectively. The characteristics of the respondents were analyzed from QP and shown in Table 5.1.

Table 5.1 Characteristic of workers with NIHL

	Characteristic	n	Percentage (%)
Race	Malay	219	71
	Chinese	41	13
	India	41	13
	Others	9	3
Gender	Female	30	10
	Male	280	90
Education	Primary	35	11
	Secondary	244	79
	University	31	10
Marital Status	Single	27	9
	Married	283	91
Designation	Manager	4	1
	Professional	28	9
	Technician	161	52
	Machine Operator	93	30
	Clerical /Service/Elementary	1	8
Age group	15-24	2	1
	25-34	53	17
	35-44	100	32
	45-54	155	50

From the study, almost all workers whom affected by excessive noise in the manufacturing of basic metals were male

(99%), followed by chemicals and paper industries. Table 5.2 shows workers with NIHL by type of industries and gender.

Table 5.2 Workers by industrial classification

Table 15 Gender of workers by type of industry

Industrial Classification	Male		Female	
	n	%	N	%
Manufacture of food products	23	7.4%	1	0.3%
Manufacture of tobacco products	25	8.1%	4	1.3%
Manufacture of textiles	24	7.7%	6	1.9%
Manufacture of wearing apparel	22	7.1%	7	2.3%
Manufacture of wood products except furniture	2	0.6%	1	0.3%
Manufacture of paper and paper products	30	9.7%	2	0.6%
Manufacture of refined petroleum products	23	7.4%	0	0.0%
Manufacture of chemicals and chemical products	34	11.0%	1	0.3%
Manufacture of other non-metallic mineral products	5	1.6%	0	0.0%
Manufacture of basic metals	75	24.2%	1	0.3%
Manufacture of fabricated metal products	12	3.9%	3	1.0%
Manufacture of motor vehicles	7	2.3%	2	0.6%

*Based on Malaysia Standard of Industrial Classification, 2008

The respondents were classified based on Malaysia Standard Classification of Occupation, 2008 which involved five (5) levels of employment; managers (1.3%), professionals (9%), technicians (52%), machine operators (30%) and service (1%). Technicians with more the 10 years working in an extreme noise exposure were among the highest risks of occupations as in Table 5.3.

Table 5.3 Designation and working experience of workers

Designation	1-2 years n (%)	6 - 10 years n (%)	11 - 20 years n (%)	21 – 30 years n (%)	> 30 years n (%)
Manager	0 (0.0%)	1 (0.3%)	3 (1.0%)	0 (0.0%)	0 (0.0%)
Professional	6 (2.0%)	0 (0.0%)	7 (2.3%)	12 (4.0%)	3 (1.0%)
Technician	11 (3.5%)	28 (9.0%)	77 (25.0%)	34 (11.0%)	13 (4.2%)
Machine Operator	12 (4.0%)	11 (3.5%)	37 (12.0%)	24 (7.7%)	7 (2.3%)
Clerical /Service/Elementary	3 (1.0%)	2 (0.6%)	14 (4.5%)	3 (1.0%)	2 (0.5%)

*Occupation based on Malaysia Standard Classification of Occupation, 2008

During the interview, an average of 25% of workers admit that they experienced symptoms of hearing loss as in Figure 5.1. However, some of them felt that having hearing loss is a stigma among the workers.

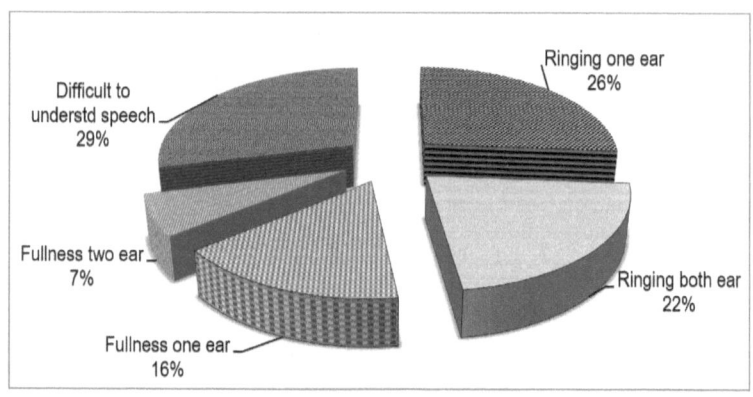

Figure 5.1 Symptom of hearing loss among manufacturing workers

5.3 STATUS OF TREATMENT AND REHABILITATION

Out of the 310 respondents, only 20% (63) workers with NIHL were referred to ENT Specialist for treatment and rehabilitation while the rest of 80% (247) need to follow up for re-assessment of audiometric test. At the time of the interview conducted, workers were still waiting for their schedule to be referring for re-assessment and further treatment at the medical care. Hence, the researcher decided to exclude those workers in the cost estimation for treatment and rehabilitation.

Based on the 63 workers referred to medical centre, 68% of them went to private medical centre that were provided by the employers as the panel medical facilities. The other 32% went to government hospitals mainly for rehabilitations and hearing aids but they also need to undergo reassessment of audiometric and consultations. Through observation, the researcher found that workers diagnosed with NIHL were discriminated by their colleagues. This is why 70% of them were not getting hearing aids as proposed by the ENT practitioner. Despite their hearing defects, more than 70% of the workers went to get medical care by their own transport. Motorbike seems to be most popular transportation. Element related with referral to the medical centre is as Table 5.4.

Table 5.4 Respondents referred to Medical Centre

	Status	n = 63	Percentage (%)
Type of Medical Centre	Government	20	80
	Private	43	20
Type of care	Consultation only	6	10
	Audiometric test only	5	8
	Consultation + Audiometric	52	82
Transportation	Own	45	71
	Others	18	29
Hearing aids proposed	No	44	70
	Yes	19	30

On the other hands, none of the respondents undergo for traditional and complementary medicines for treatment of NIHL.

5.4 COST OF NIHL

In the context of this study, the total cost includes direct costs and indirect costs. Both of these costs are borne by the three parties associated with NIHL disease of workers, employers and government.

Direct costs were included financing the medical care and transportation for treatment of NIHL. In this study, the occupational health doctors or medical practitioners reviewed the on-site audiometric results. Then, workers with severe hearing impairment at high frequency were referred to the ENT Specialist for further examination and treatment with regard of the employer's medical panel.

Most of the employers pay for the medical costs, but there are situation that workers produced their own pocket money. Workers whom seek treatment at the government hospital only pay RM5.00 fee for service. The real cost of medical care and hearing aids to be borne by the government. On the other hand, employers provide an audiometric testing program for the workers as required by the Factories and Machinery (Noise Exposure) Regulations 1986.

However, indirect costs were involved loss of time that has been spent for medical treatment and attending the audiometric testing in the workplace. Hearing conservation training is also included as non-productive time that the workers were not doing their routine job. Employer sometimes needs to find replacement of workers with NIHL and in a certain circumstances; they need to pay for overtime. For every occupational NIHL cases reported to both government agencies; the Department of Occupational Safety and Health and the Social Security Organization, investigations will be conducted and an amount of benefit will be paid to the workers with hearing defects.

5.5 COST OF NIHL BY WORKERS AND EMPLOYERS

Based on the analysis, the mean cost was analyzed according to the survey finding from workers and employers as in Table 5.5. However, the figure was adjusted and round up in the results.

Table 5.5 Cost of NIHL borne by the workers and employer

	N	Mean (RM)	Std. Dev.	Min	Max
Cost by workers					
Medical care	36	111.67	122.72	5.00	600.00
Transportation	45	19.50	12.38	10.00	60.00
Loss of time for medical care	63	47.99	30.42	8.30	134.20
Loss of time for onsite audiometric	63	13.04	-	4.17	26.04
Loss of time for awareness training	63	91.26	-	29.17	182.29
Cost by employers					
Medical Care (private)	12	224.17	142.08	100.00	500.00
Onsite audiometric	25	64.00	36.58	15.00	150.00
Transportation	5	42.00	37.68	10.00	100.00
Job replacement	13	88.46	-	95.85	287.50
Overtime	40	239.58	-	47.92	239.58
Days of sick leave	12	1.25	0.87	1.00	4.00

5.6 COST OF NIHL BORNE BY THE WORKER

The total mean cost of NIHL by the workers is RM287.00. 46.0 % (RM131.00 per case) is direct cost that consists of medical care and transportation; and 54.0 % of indirect cost comprises of loss of productive time for medical care, onsite audiometric and hearing conservation training.

Through out the survey of 310 workers, only one of them accompanied by the spouse during medical care and rehabilitation but the finding is ignored because the figure is minority and does not represent the caregivers.

5.6.1 Direct Cost Of NIHL Borne By Worker

i) Cost for medical care

In overall, the mean cost for medical care is RM111.67 (SD122.72) per worker. The workers undergone medical treatment for NIHL divided into two groups. The first group was 20 workers whom seek medical care at the government hospital. Nineteen (19) of them use their out of pocket except one person used retirement guarantee facility to pay the medical care expenses. The mean cost for medical care at the government hospital was RM48.42 with minimum charges was only RM5.00 and maximum as high as RM130.00 per visit. All workers receive the same treatment for NIHL; pure tone audiometry (PTA) and Tympanometry. This was confirmed by the ENT report from Unit Audiology, Jabatan Othorinolaringology of Hospital Tengku Ampuan Rahimah Klang.

On the other hand, 43 workers get medical care for NIHL from the private medical centre and 17 of them paid with their own money and 14 of them use medical card facility provided by the company. The mean cost for private medical care is RM182.35 per visit with minimum charges of RM50.00 and maximum charges of RM600.00. The researcher was unable to access the private medical record, which was kept as confidential by the Human Resource Department of each company. The researcher assumes that the treatment of NIHL received by the workers is the same treatment given by the government hospital.

ii) Cost for transportation

The mean cost for two-way journey from the workplace to medical center was RM19.50 (SD12.38). Despite the employer provide company transport, more than 70.0% of the workers use their own transport to get medical treatment and their fuel consumption cost ranged between RM10.00 and RM60.00 per journey.

5.6.2 Indirect Cost Of NIHL By Worker

i) Cost for loss of productive time for medical treatment

The average time spend at the medical centre is 3.5 hours per treatment (min: 2 hours & max: 9 hours). The mean cost of work replacement is RM47.99 (SD30.42) when all the respective workers were not performing their routine work in the production.

ii) Cost for loss of productive time for onsite audiometric

The workers also spend an average of one hour of their productive time attending the onsite audiometric test. The cost of time loss was based on each workers monthly salary and the mean cost of time loss for onsite audiometric is RM15.00 per test.

iii) Cost for work loss for hearing conservation training

In accordance to the requirement by the Noise Regulation 1986, every worker must attend hearing conservation training. For the purpose of this research the training was based on the one-day NIOSH standard syllabus. The mean cost of time loss is RM93.00 per training session per worker.

5.7 COST OF NIHL BORNE BY THE EMPLOYER

The total mean costs of NIHL borne by the employer are RM998.00. Direct cost spend was reasonable at RM330.00 per case for medical care, onsite audiometric and transportation. While, indirect costs expenditure were so much higher with 67.0% (RM668.00) of the total mean costs, which included cost of job replacement, overtime, sick leave and training.

5.7.1 Direct cost of NIHL by employer

i) Cost for medical care

The employer funded 12 out of 43 workers with NIHL to the private medical centre. The mean cost for medical care is RM224.17(SD142.08) per visit per worker. The researcher does not include the amount of insurance premium paid by the company due to scarce of data within OSH practitioners in the industries.

ii) Cost for transportation

The mean cost for journey to the medical centre and back to the industry is RM42.00 (SD37.68) per visit.

iii) Cost for onsite-audiometric test

The mean cost of onsite audiometric test is RM64.00 (SD36.58) is based on 25 industries that appointed service providers, else one company has in-house audiometric booth with no service charges. The charges for onsite audiometric test ranged from RM15.00 to RM150.00 per worker, depending on the location of the industrial area and the qualification of the medical officer reviewed the audiogram.

5.7.2 Indirect cost of NIHL borne by employer

i) Cost for job replacement

The employers were also burdened to replace workers while the one with NIHL went to get medical care. Job replacement reported were only 13 cases, which has costs, the employer RM88.46 per replacement. The cost was calculated from the average monthly salary for 24 working days of the non-productive time spend.

ii) Cost for overtime

The implication of having NIHL treatment is not only time to be replaced by other workers but also overtime job. In this study, the employer paid about of RM480.00 for 40 hours overtime. The mean cost of overtime is RM239.58.

iii) Cost for sick leave

The medical practitioner provided a total of 12 days of sick leave for treatment that has caused loss of productive time. The mean cost for loss of time for sick leave is RM179.83 (SD175.25).

iv) Cost for hearing conservation training

The researcher referred to the standard training scheme at NIOSH Malaysia. The in-house hearing conservation-training package costs RM4000.00 per day for 25 people. Thus, the average cost for training per workers is RM160.00.

5.8 COST OF NIHL BY GOVERNMENT

5.8.1 Direct cost of NIHL by government

i) Cost for medical care

The cost of medical care by the government hospital was collected from a secondary data at the International Centre for Casemix and Clinical Coding, UKM Medical Centre (2010). The mean cost is RM272.00 per patient, was based on a top down costing for outpatient in the Department Of Surgical And Medical clinic. The researcher assumed that the cost of outpatient cases in the Ear, Nose and Throat Clinics are compatible with the estimated cost for the Surgical And Medical Clinic.

ii) Cost of rehabilitation

Rehabilitation of NIHL requires the use of hearing aid to the workers affected. The price of hearing aids varies from as low as RM2000.00 per piece to as high as RM6000.00 per piece for the casual communication purposes. In this country, workers were protected by the Social Security Act, which financially helps the workers for hearing rehabs. The average cost of hearing aid is RM4000.00 were referred to the Rehabilitation Unit, Social Security Organization Kuala Lumpur,

5.8.2 Indirect cost of NIHL borne by government

i) Cost of investigation

A routine investigation was carried out for NIHL cases reported to both authorities; DOSH and SOCSO. The researcher estimated the investigation cost through an observation of the flow of investigation work process according to the MS ISO 9002 in both agencies that includes salary of staffs, the length of time for each task, meetings, report writing, travelling allowances as in Table 5.6 & 5.7. The mean cost of investigation is RM120.00 per case per year for task implemented by DOSH and RM523.00 per case per year by SOCSO.

Table 5.6 Cost of investigation per NIHL case by DOSH

Designation	Task time (hour/case)	Salary per hour (RM)	Investigation cost (RM)
Admin Officer	0.17	9.00	1.00
Dep. Director	0.67	44.00	30.00
Head Section	0.67	40.00	27.00
Investigation Officer	8.00	21.00	52.00
Travelling time	0.13	21.00	3.00
Travelling Allowances			7.00
Total cost of DOSH			120.00

* Figures has been rounded

Table 5.6 Cost of investigation per NIHL case by SOCSO

Designation	Task time (hour/case)	Salary per hour (RM)	Investigation cost (RM)
Admin Officer	2.33	21.88	51.00
Investigation Officer	5.00	28.13	141.00
Executive Officer	0.83	34.38	56.00
Travelling allowances			29.00
Sr. Executive Officer	0.83	43.75	36.00
Medical Board Management staff			90.00
Medical Board Panel allowance			120.00
Total cost of SOCSO			523.00

* Figures has been rounded

ii) Cost of occupational disease benefit

SOCSO managed permanent disablement due to occupational disease by referring to the Second Schedule of Employee Social Security Act. Based on the data from Occupational Health Division of SOCSO Kuala Lumpur, the average cost for the benefit paid by SOCSO to the worker with NIHL is RM26,500.00 per case in the same year.

5.9 TOTAL ECONOMIC BURDEN OF NIHL IN MALAYSIA

5.9.1 Total direct cost of NIHL

The average total direct cost of NIHL shared by the worker, employer and government was RM4733.00 comprises of medical care (RM608), on-site audiometric (RM64), rehabilitation (RM4000) and transportation (RM61). The government bears almost 90% (RM4272) of the total direct cost for mainly for benefit payment, whilst, the employer shared only 7% (RM330) and worker are at the minimum of 3% (RM131).

5.9.2 Total indirect cost of NIHL

The total indirect cost of NIHL is RM27,967.00 that includes loss of productive time (RM664); training packages by the employer (RM160); investigation by DOSH and SOCSO (RM643); and benefit payment by SOCSO (RM26500). Once again, government bears the biggest share of cost with 97% (RM27143) from the total indirect cost, followed by employer 2.4% (RM668) and worker 0.6% (RM156).

5.9.3 Total cost of NIHL

The average total cost of NIHL was RM32,700.00 and on the overall, the cost of NIHL was significantly higher for the government (96%) then employer (3%) and the worker (1%) as showed in Table 22. In overall, the indirect expenditures by the government are significant to the direct costs compared to the workers and employers as in Figure 9.

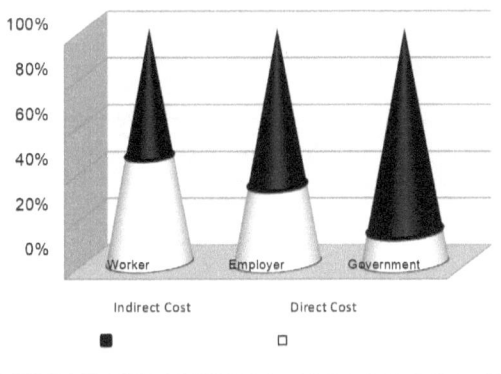

Figure 5.2 Comparison of direct and indirect expenditures

Table 5.7 Total cost of NIHL per worker per year

Cost component	Total Cost (RM)	Cost of NIHL per worker per year (RM)		
		Worker W	Employer E	Government G
DIRECT COST				
Medical Care & Rehab	4672			
Medical care	608	112	224	272
Onsite audiometric	64		64	
Rehabilitation - hearing aids	4000			4000
Transportation	61			
Transportation	61	19	42	
Total Direct Cost	4733			
INDIRECT COST				
Loss of productivity time	664			
Loss of time for medical care	48	48		
Loss of time for onsite audiometric	15	15		
Loss of time for awareness training	93	93		
Job replacement	88		88	
Overtime	240		240	
Sick leave	180		180	
Training	160			
Annual awareness training	160		160	
Investigation & Benefit expenditure	27143			
Investigation procedures	643			643
Benefit expenditure	26500			26500
Total Indirect Cost	27967			
TOTAL COST				
Total burden by W, E, G		287	998	31415
Percentage of burden by W, E, G (%)		1%	3%	96%
TOTAL ANNUAL BURDEN	32700			

5.10 THE NATIONAL ECONOMIC BURDEN OF NIHL

Based on the estimated number of potential workers with NIHL (103673) as mentioned in Chapter 4 and the average total cost of NIHL (RM32700), the national economic burden of NIHL was RM3,390,107,100.00 that makes 0.36% of the Gross Domestic Product (GDP) of 2012.

5.11 SCENARIO-BASED SENSITIVITY ANALYSIS

Further analysis was carried out to determine if the trend for the total workers with NIHL change would result in the significant changes of the total cost of NIHL and percentage of GDP. This analysis is crucial to identify the possibility of financial impact when the existing noise regulation is reviewed. In this sensitivity analysis, three scenarios were assumed; base case, best case and worse case scenario as in Table 23.

5.11.1 Base case scenario

The base case scenario considered the total workforce in the manufacturing sectors of 103, 673 workers in complying the existing noise regulations. The total cost of NIHL was RM3,390,107,100.00 for of workers with NIHL at 0.38% of GDP.

5.11.2 Best case scenario

Assumption of the best scenario was when the total workers with NIHL reduced 25% to 77755. The total cost of NIHL was RM2,542,580,325.00 and percentage of GDP was lower at

0.29%. This scenario can materialized when all manufacturing industries affected with excessive noise implement effective hearing conservation program that was one of the targeted program in the National OSH Mater Plan 2015 by DOSH.

5.11.3 Worse case scenario

In the worse case scenario, the total workers with NIHL increased 25% to 129591 with the cost of NIHL RM4,237,633,875.00 at 0.48% of GDP. The increment was assumed when no preventive action were taken to allocate appropriate control measures of the existing noise sources. Moreover, the same scenario will also occur when the existing noise regulation is reviewed and the scope is expanded to other economic sectors. The new regulation will widened their scope of economic sector as in Occupational Safety and Health Act (1994).

Table 5.8 Scenario based Sensitivity Analysis

Sensitivity analysis	Scenario 1	Scenario 2	Scenario 3
Type of Scenario	BASE	BEST	WORSE
Total cost of NIHL	RM32,700.00	RM32,700.00	RM32,700.00
No. of potential workers with NIHL	103673	77755	129591
Total annual burden of NIHL	RM3,390,107,100.00	RM2,542,580,325.00	RM4,237,633,875.00
Total annual burden by % of GDP	0.4%	0.3%	0.5%

CHAPTER VI

DISCUSSION

6.1 INTRODUCTION

This chapter discusses the gaps of the literature and the important findings of the study, through to the results obtained. The main objective of the study is to estimate the economic burden of NIHL in the manufacturing industries in Malaysia. This study was undertaken to forecast the number of workers potential with NIHL and estimated average cost of NIHL by the employer, worker as well as the government. A scenario-based comparison was performed to give a bigger picture of the financial implication if NIHL were to be at worst condition.

6.2 PROPORTION OF POTENTIAL WORKERS WITH NIHL

In this study, the percentage of potential workers with NIHL in each type of manufacturing was based on the data collected from the OSH practitioners and extrapolated to the total workers population in the economic census for respective industry. Data were referred to the total workers exposed to noise more than 85dBA based on the area noise monitoring results conducted in the work area.

The area noise monitoring reported the level of noise exposure at specific point of noise source in the work area. The number of workers exposed was counted from the total number of employees by departments that involved in the working area.

Assumption was made from the data collected were all workers exposed have already affected with NIHL. There is uncertainty in estimates of the proportion of workers that were having NIHL, however, the assumption used has not been tested and a deeper survey and more stringent enforcement would give better results and improve the uncertainty.

6.3 DEMOGRAPHY DATA OF WORKERS WITH NIHL

The data recorded by the Occupational Health Division, DOSH Putrajaya provides the characteristics of the workers with NIHL in manufacturing industries in Malaysia. The manufacturing industries were the major industry affected with excessive noise (NIOSH USA 2009). A study on the prevalence of NIHL among textile workers in Kashim Bazar, Gazipur was 33.46% (Haider 2008).

The NIHL data indicated mostly male (90%) workers aged more than 45 years old (50%) were dominantly affected with NIHL in this industry. This has been investigated by Palmer et al. (2001) in Great Britain.

In this study, technician and machine operator were the highest (82%) group of occupations with NIHL. Waitzman & Smith (1998) also found the blue collar workers were at higher risk (two to more than 3 fold) of hearing loss in construction industries compared to white collar and clerical staffs.

Workers with NIHL were sampled purely based on the audiogram result from the on-site audiometric test. Hearing loss associated with cardiovascular risk such as hypertension (Kempen et. al 2002) and other factors that may contribute to NIHL such as chemicals, ototoxic drugs and vibrations (Campbell 2004) were not considered.

Another important findings in hearing loss are annoyance feeling from noise. In Western Europe, Australia and the USA, studies have been carried out on noise-based annoyance, which interferes someone's thoughts, feelings or daily activities, which resulted a feeling of resentment, displeasure, discomfort, dissatisfaction or offence (Vermeer 1993). Unfortunately, there is no demand to compare this situation in Malaysia.

6.4 HEARING CONSERVATION PROGRAM IN MANUFACTURING INDUSTRY

Hearing conservation program is one of the requirements in the noise regulation enforced in this country. Despite the compliance of the legislation, evidence on HCP to effective intervention is still lacking (Verbeek et al. 2009). Goelzer (2001) recommended that hearing conservation program should be an integrations of overall hazard prevention and control mechanism that requires political will, decision making from employers and commitments from both parties; the top management and workers. However, a local study in Negeri Sembilan concluded that there were no relation between the hearing loss and hearing conservation program implemented (Nur saleha 2009).

6.4.1 Hearing protection device as noise control

In this era of modern industry, the owners invested on purchasing high-tech machinery, putting a high hope of producing a quality output and making higher profit. Yet, some of the machines were not equipped with sound absorbers or dampers and need engineering control treatment to be able to control noise while working.

Typically, a large industry has adequate financial provisions for occupational safety and health (OSH) such as noise engineering control. However, recommendation for engineering control by the enforcement officer is a nightmare for a medium industry that has limited budget for OSH.

A common misconception among employers associated with effective noise control is when each employee to wear hearing protection devices. Meanwhile, the primary responsibility of the employer is controlling noise through the control hierarchy that describes the use of hearing protection devices in the final stages of control.

In this study, the last hierarchy of control of wearing hearing protection device (HPD) is the most popular among employers. All employers provide workers with HPD according to their needs whether earplugs or earmuff. There are also employers who provide both, for complete protection.

Inefficient of control measures and unsuitable hearing protection devices (HPD) impacted their hearing. In addition, the workers may still lacking of knowledge on noise exposure effects and the correct way of wearing HPD, the maintenance of HPD and upmost important their personal hygiene when dealing with HPD.

In addition, under-used hearing protection (Tak et al. 2009) and differential use of protectors between the situations (Rabinowitz et al. 2007) be the reasons to higher rate of hearing loss in a moderate noise area than in an excessive noise area.

Previous studies highlighted on the behavior, attitudes, and beliefs and consistency of the workers wearing HPD with education principles (Caffarella 1994; Merriam 1993). Lusk et al. (2003) found that annual training provided by the employer are significant but in small progress towards achieving a constant use of HPDs. An intervention delivered consistently between 6 to 18 months prior to the audiometric test showed changes of behavior from difficult-to-influence ones.

Further study on the psychological disturbance of the workers wearing HPDs at longer period of time and uncomfortable condition such as hot work environment should be carried out to introduce suitable culture at the right working condition.

6.4.2 ATTENUATION OF HEARING PROTECTION DEVICE

The main expectation when using hearing protection devices (HPDs) is to reduce noise exposures to acceptable levels that can protect workers effectively (Edwards and Green 1987; Savell and Toothman 1987; Bruhl and Ivarsson 1994). Normally, effective HPDs were used upon training (Toivonen et al. 2002), giving feedbacks (Zohar et. al 1980) and enforcement (Hager et. al 1982).

All hearing protectors in the market were labeled with a noise reduction rating (NRR). NRR is an estimate of the amount of attenuation that a particular hearing protector provides when fitted but it does not adequately control for real-world variability in attenuation (Berger et al. 1998). The best estimate is a measurement of attenuation on an individual (Personal Attenuation Rating- PAR) in the real world that depends on individual-specific HPD fit.

Through out the survey, all the 26 industries provide HPDs labeled with NRR but none of them measures PAR of the workers. The researcher in opinion that having an estimate of PAR to every worker wearing HPDs will help to determine the factor of hearing loss due to ineffective use of HPDs.

6.4.3 Audiometric Testing Program

The Factories and Machinery (Noise Exposure) Regulations 1989 requires employer to conduct audiometric test to all workers exposed more than permissible level. The researcher observed few contributing factors to inefficient of audiometric testing program at the place of work.

DOSH functioned to give approval to operate the mobile audiometric units. Current record shows that there are 115 units of audiometric test centre including the mobile unit through out the nation. The ratio of workers with NIHL to the number of mobile units was obviously small. OSH practitioners remarked the difficulties in obtaining audiometric test service at a required time, which caused a delay in measuring worker's impairment.

Besides, limited units of mobile audiometric, the industrial location was a side factors for the service providers. For example, an industry located about 85km away from Kuantan town in Pahang reported to be left out and extended their waiting time for nearly one year to get the service. This has been non-compliance to the existing noise regulations.

The researcher also received complaints from the workers regarding the condition of the mobile audiometric vehicles that were not up to the standards. During the test, the workers can hear sound from outside of the unit. Based on the researcher's experience in enforcement of the Noise Regulation 1989, the situation might be caused by the unsuitable location of the mobile unit, for example near a busy road or inappropriate insulation of the mobile unit. Both of these reason will impacted the audiometric results.

Other factor is stigmatism of deaf workers that was popular among those whom need to undergo the audiometric testing. Through out the survey, in general, the workers were psychologically affected when they were seen to queue for the test during working hours. In fact, there are female workers whom do not want to admit that they have hearing impairment. They were lip reading while being interviewed by the researcher and more prefer to answer the questionnaires. In avoidance of the stigma, there are possibilities that workers were not answering the audiometric test correctly that resulted inaccurate audiogram.

Seeing the real situation of the audiometric services in the field, the researcher was in favor that an urgent need to review the existing regulation to furnish a comprehensive industrial code of practice on occupational hearing conservation program to the employer and service providers. Parallel to that, the OSH Master Plan was targeting more service provider to help the industry to access hearing level among their affected workers by 2015 (OSH MP 2015).

6.5 INPUT TO THE REGULATORY IMPACT ANALYSIS (RIA)

Although occupational NIHL is the most popular occupational disease around the globe but there is limited study that investigated on the financial spending by the workers with NIHL, the employer whom manage NIHL and the government that give services on NIHL. Many studies are based mainly on the cost of occupational accidents and noise control interventions but the conclusion may not be applied to estimate financial implication due to occupational disease.

An analysis of cost in this study indicated that the cost of NIHL was lower when there is less number of potential workers with NIHL. Increase of awareness on hearing conservation and appropriate attitude in protection their hearing among workers may be the reducing factors of NIHL but Dobie R. (2008) in his study on NIHL burden in United State remarked more stringent enforcement of noise exposure during work will probably reduced the burden of NIHL.

The cost of occupational NIHL is essential to determine any appropriate options when reviewing existing legislation on the effectiveness and efficient. In Malaysia, a good regulatory practice requires a structured approach that evaluates the costs and benefits systematically.

The Regulatory Impact Analysis (RIA) is implemented to examine the likely impacts on the proposed new regulation in comparison to alternative options that could meet the government's objective. A comprehensive assessment of the impacts of the costs and benefits for each feasible option were conducted in consideration of the existing regulation as the baseline. The assessment will provide the decision maker on the likely merits of the feasible options. The costs and benefits were the term used in RIA as to describe the positive and negative effects of a proposal that should cover business or the employer, consumer and the government.

In fact, this study covers a relatively broad scope of research that involves three main components in the manufacturing of employers, employees and the government. However, the researchers were determined in obtaining data and information for this study in order to contribute to the to the selection of economical option for noise exposure enforcement. Such study should be carried out consistently in every five years to review the effectiveness of enforcement in respect of regulatory requirements.

This study was done in a timely manner, in which the RIA is required to review the existing Factories and Machinery (Noise Exposure) Regulations 1989. For a developing country like Malaysia, the impact of legislation on the employer is an important consideration to avoid economic pressures of earnings among industrial players. The authority must give priority to the industries in order to review existing regulation or making new ones.

The results of the study on economic burden of NIHL at the manufacturing industries were the crucial data required for the impact assessment. The unit cost of each cost component was derived from this study. Unfortunately, this study does not explore the type of control measure or noise intervention implemented in the industries to reduce the noise exposure level including usage of hearing protection device. The cost of each enclosure type control, size 4' X 5' is approximately RM30,000.00 for the stamping machine. This is the real burden to the industries exposed to excessive noise risk at the workplace.

Usage of HPD was in the last hierarchy of control and as an interim or additional worker's protection from noise exposure, hence any cost of control measures were not consider in this research.

Despite the direct and indirect costs, from the survey, OSH practitioners at the 26 industries responded that the productivity loss due to NIHL was insignificant. In fact, there is no record regarding NIHL loss of productive time. However, in order to complete the impact analysis, the researcher suggested taking secondary data from a study on net-cost model of engineering noise control in Singapore (Lahiri et.al 2011).

6.6 THE AVERAGE MEDICAL CARE COSTS

The outcome of this study indicated that in overall, the government spends more as compared to the employer and workers in managing occupational NIHL. The average medical care cost for the government is slightly higher than the employer. It was a secondary data, averaged from the survey to the OSH practitioner and the estimated from the top down costing and assumed from the surgery clinic by the ITCC UKMMC. The real costs should consider the same type of treatment and rehabilitation received by the worker with NIHL. Unfortunately, due to confidentiality of records, the researcher could not access the information of treatment during the survey.

Reporting of occupational disease is an obligation to all employer and medical practitioner. Every medical practitioner or medical officer attending to, or called in to visit, a patient whom he believes to be suffering from any of the occupational poisoning or occupational disease listed in Third Schedule or

Table 16, must report the matter to the Director General within 7 days using the approved form (JKKP 7) (NADOPOD, 2004). Under this requirement, the total reported cases to DOSH comprise of employer's report as well as suspected NIHL cases, which still need further confirmation. This is the reason of why the number of referred NIHL cases is relatively small compared to the total respondent.

6.7 CONSIDERATIONS ON CONFOUNDING FACTORS OF NIHL

The facts that an employee is suffering from NIHL likely originate from a variety of ancillary factors other than exposure to noise at work. Increased hearing loss can be resulted from the environment noise outside the workplace which is difficult to determine. In fact, the investigation of this scenario is not possible because it may require large capital outlays and basically almost impossible to implement. In addition, the diagnosis of NIHL is complicated due to the contributory causes of noise exposure that are not from workplace such as recreation (Marlenga et al. 2012); consideration of lifestyle, for example cigarette smoking that has been strongly-related with an increased frequency of hearing loss (Kurmis 2007), usage of ototoxic drugs or medications (Fuente 2011); undergone a surgery, having ear infections and illness; as well as genetic.

Other causes at work apart from noise exposure, that can cause NIHL is chemical reaction to the workers in the chemical manufacturing industry. A certain type of chemicals hazardous to health are potential to damage the hair cells in the inner ear. Besides, in construction industry, a prolonged exposure to acoustic vibration might caused hearing damage (Kurmis 2007).

Apart of the medical examination procedures, in the pre-screening of audiometric testing, questions regarding personal backgrounds; working experience; past medical history and hobby were asked but the results were unlikely to be explored in terms of academic study. But, there is constraint among medical practitioners to confirm any occupational related disease or occupational NIHL except NIHL cases referred by SOCSO are easier to confirm.

In Malaysia, the occupational health issues were not a priority as compared to public health cases that caused limited information on the occupational disease data in the national disease database. The result of this study was only based on the reported NIHL case in compliance of Factories and Machinery (Noise Exposure) Regulation 1989 that does not consider any of the confounding factors of NIHL.

6.8 STUDY STRENGTH AND LIMITATIONS

The main strength of this study is the method used and the source of data collected. Although the objective of this study seems simple, data for this study were collected from three different types of respondents, that involved 310 workers who reported suffering from NIHL in the manufacturing industries, then, interviews to 26 OSH practitioners whom representing employers and lastly, the government officers included five DOSH officers, two SOCSO officers and a lecturer from UKMMC.

Firstly, in estimating the number of potential workers with NIHL, effort were made to investigate the noise management practices implemented in the workplace and the status of noise exposure among workers in the industries. A thorough review in the current economic census was conducted to obtain the total employment in the manufacturing industry. Combining the findings from the survey and information from the census yielded the overall output in estimating potential NIHL cases among manufacturing industrial workers.

In estimating the cost of NIHL by the employers, this study has selected all manufacturing industries with NIHL cases that reported to DOSH and stratified the respondents randomly into four regions in Peninsular Malaysia. The effort ensures that all type of manufacturing industries identified with excessive noise was sampled accordingly.

The study tool were modified from the industrial accident cost calculator practiced by DOSH that is also a study strength that allowed the researcher to estimate the costs after having NIHL that makes the findings reliable. In addition, a scenario-based analysis were included to describe best scenario in terms of percentage to the GDP and assist for best option for the regulatory impact assessment.

In overall, several limitations in this study identified that may interfere its findings. First, findings on the cost of medical care ranges from RM5.00 to RM600.00 each NIHL case. Normally, government hospital charges were lower that the private medical centre. However, the information on treatment and rehabilitation from the medical record could not be drawn. Medical records for worker referred to private medical centre were kept confidential at the centre. But, for workers refer to the government hospital, the medical record is well kept at the human resource department and is available during the survey. The unavailable records have created a gap between the cost of private medical centre and the cost of government hospital, that it should be the similar type of treatment. Nonetheless, data of medical care from the top down costing at the surgery clinic UKMMC has somehow averaged the cost of medical care at the government hospital.

Another limitation of this study is the method of obtaining data from the workers. Initially, the intention was questionnaires guided face-to-face interviews to all 310 workers. However, due to the difficulties in arranging the work shifts and limited time approved by the management of the industry, instead of individual face-to-face, the interviews had to be performed in group of 10 to 15 workers with a general briefing on the questionnaires. Each worker experienced a question and answer session upon delivering the questionnaires to the researcher. There are questions in the questionnaires need the workers to remember the frequency and amount spend by them. To limit the biasness, the researcher refer to Human Resource Department as a guide to frequency and amount spend for NIHL cases.

CHAPTER VII
CONCLUSION AND RECOMMENDATIONS

7.1 CONCLUSION AND STUDY FINDINGS

This is a rare and unique study conducted for occupational NIHL in Malaysia. Although NIHL is one of the highest reported occupational disease cases, information on the disease were not properly compiled and analyzed. Method on the management of NIHL was already documented as in the Guidelines of Management of Occupational NIHL published by Ministry of Health. The existing noise regulation (1989) limits the enforcement scope only to factory and does not cover other industrial sector i.e agriculture, public sector, utilities and etc. Hence, there is a gap in the enforcement of OSH law in Malaysia. In order to review the existing regulation, a concrete justification is required with evidence to be presented in the Regulatory Impact Statement. The assessment for the statement is called Regulatory Impact Assessment (RIA) that need two major components in it, the cost of NIHL and the scenario

87

based sensitivity analysis. Therefore, this study provides both of the components through on the basis of the economic burden of occupational NIHL among manufacturing industrial workers complete with details of direct and indirect cost components. The result shows a significant percentage on the potential workers with NIHL from the gross domestic product based.

An interesting study which promotes the involvement of the OSH practitioner and workers through interviews and questionnaires; reviews and observations on working procedures for occupational health section, DOSH and review of procedures for benefits management by SOCSO. It opens the opportunity for the OSH practitioner to understand more about noise exposure and the obligation to the employer.

The requirement on reporting of occupational diseases has encouraged the employer and medical practitioners to report NIHL cases to the authority. This study found that some of NIHL cases were diagnosed based on site audiometric results and some were confirmed after referring to the medical centre. The weakness was in the existing reporting system that requires the medical practitioners to report not only confirmed cases but also suspected cases increased the number of cases. However, the shortage of audiometric service providers creates delayed in identification of hearing loss in which some of workers had severe hearing loss at the point audiometric test were conducted. In addition, lack of knowledge and understanding on hearing conservation among the OSH practitioners are among the possible reasons for the underreporting of NIHL cases. It is recommended that the existing flow of occupational NIHL notification by Ministry of Health to be incorporated in the existing Guidelines on Safety and Health (Notification of Accident, Dangerous Occurrence, Occupational Poisoning and

Occupational Disease) Regulations 2004 [NADOPOD] and should be established to overcome the setbacks of managing NIHL at the place of work.

During the survey, majority of the respondent have no knowledge of the level of noise exposure at their workplace. All they know are they needed to wear ear protection while at work. Some showed their commitment to protect hearing and use defect earplug (faded colour and mold). Even though, ear protection are supplied and used, the truth is that the workers are not train on how to use hearing protection properly. In the employer's perspective, the annual awareness training attended by the workers working in excessive noise was enough to create self-awareness. There is an increase of health awareness after workers attended training on self-care in order to reduce and prevent work-related accidents, injuries and illnesses (Arphorn et. al 2010). In addition to this, the worker's knowledge need to be enhance with a regularly alerts to their true occupational noise exposures from the hazard signage, best practice, spot the hazard and many other interactive activities. This regular caution from the OSH practitioners will encourage them to improve their skill on the effective use the HPD and in a consistent manner. Indirectly, by understanding the noise exposure and enhancement of skill using HPD, the workers are able to avoid unnecessarily sources of loud noise at work.

At the point of this study ended, the Industrial Code of Practice on hearing conservation program (ICOP) was in progress to be published. It is recommended a comprehensive approach in order to train the workers to understand their working environment should be included in the ICOP. Thee ICOP is known to furnish the new noise regulations with regards all emerging issues found in this study.

7.2 MAIN CONTRIBUTION OF THIS STUDY

This study have successfully estimates the average cost of NIHL from three perspective; workers, employers and government in Malaysia. The findings provide us a set of fresh cost evaluation in the case of NIHL for a worker in a year. There is very limited information in the current literature since NIHL is not a major health concern among the community as to compared to other disease outbreak. At this time, there is complete evidence on the cost of NIHL and analysis on the worse case scenario of NIHL to justify the review of existing Noise Regulation (1989).

7.3 RECOMMENDATION AND FUTURE RESEARCH

Occupational NIHL in Malaysia graphed a consistent rise since decades ago, but very few study were found to investigate the impact of existing enforcement system. The OSH Master Plan 2015 targeted a regulatory impact analysis to be performed to estimate the costs and benefits of NIHL. The results of this study have complimented the required data for the analysis except for the benefits components.

The top management meeting of DOSH Malaysia, chaired by the Director General on June 2014, has endorsed the results and findings as an important input for the impact assessment. Further to that, it is recommended that a cost calculator for NIHL be developed in separate calculator for the employer and government respectively that will benefit the employer especially in selecting best option for control measure.

In order to strengthen the findings of this study, further researches should be in place. A through examination on the severity of hearing loss due to noise exposure and the confounding factors related to hearing loss such as chemicals and cigarette smoking should be conducted to furnish a more accurate hearing loss population. A study among airport workers in Malaysia demonstrate that the prevalence of hearing loss is 33.5% with consideration of age of forty and smoking habits (Nasir and Rampal 2012).

Further study on the control measure options implemented at the industries should be evaluated for average cost of different type of interventions in different class of manufacturing industries. This would enable the estimation of cost benefit analysis of preventive measures to enhance the investments among employers. There is also a need to further research on the effectiveness of the use of hearing protection device as an interim control measure, HPD fit test and the attenuation for each workers. Provision of HPD itself is not sufficient to protect the workers; hence what more important is to control the severity of hearing loss among the affected ones.

A feasibility study on the mobile audiometric service provider to test workers in urban and suburban area like Kerteh, Terengganu is worth investigating. Most of the time, industries located in the urban area were likely to get audiometric service on scheduled. While varieties of costs quoted to the employers, there are still lacking on the availability service provider when it is needed ones. A real time investigation should be performed to understand the restraint faced by them.

Finally, to further establish the potential employment with NIHL, it is recommended that the same study are conducted to other sectors than manufacturing industries including agriculture, services, building construction, mining and others.

This group will actually contribute to a bigger number of NIHL cases in this country. Parallel to the national agenda of OSH, a net economic model for occupational disease should be developed in preparation of self-regulatory culture.

7.4 OVERALL CONCLUSIONS

This study introduced new knowledge in the field of occupational health, specifically occupational noise related disease, NIHL. The study findings are best to suit the requirement of impact assessment and hoped to increase the cost consciousness among the industrial player, whom exposed excessive loud noise to their workers. It is recommended that this study should be further expanding to other sectors that also exposed risk of hearing loss to the workers. The national economic burden of NIHL was projected to higher if all the other industrial sectors (agriculture, transportation etc.) were enforced. As NIHL cases imposed a substantial amount of burden on workers, employers and government in Malaysia, a more effective hearing conservation program should be in-place at the industries and more stringent enforcement should be implemented.

The findings were appropriate to furnish inputs on the cost of NIHL for the Regulatory Impact Analysis conducted by DOSH, in order to select the best solution in upgrading the existing noise regulation

BIBLIOGRAPHY

Arphorn S., Chaonasuan P., Pruktharathikul V., Singhakajen V., Chaikittiporn C. 2010. A Program for Thai Rubber Tappers to Improve the Cost of Occupational Health and Safety. *Industrial Health Journal* 48:276-282.

Asante A.F., Asenso-Okyere K., 2003. *Economic burden of Malaria in Ghana*. A technical report submitted to the World Health Organization, African Regional Office.

Ashraf H., Younus M., Kumar P., Siddiqui T., Ali S. et al. 2009. Frequency of hearing loss among textile industry workers of weaving unit in Karachi, Pakistan. *Journal of Pakistan Medical Association,* 59, 575 – 576.

B. Marlenga, R. Berg, J. Linneman et al. 2012. Determinants of early-stage hearing loss among a cohort of young workers with 16-year follow-up. *Occupational and Environment Medicine* 69:479e484

Berger EH, Franks JR, Behar A, et al., 1998. Development of a new standard laboratory protocol for estimating the field attenuation of hearing protection devices. Part III. The validity of using subject-fit data. *The Journal of Acoustical Society of America* 103:665e72

Berger E.H., Royster L.H, Royster J.D., Driscoll D.P., Layne M. 2003. *The Noise Manual*. American Industrial Hygiene Association Press.

Brian O.B. 1956. Noise in Industry. *Occupational Medicine : Oxford Journal* 109-111. http://occmed.oxfordjournals.org

Bruhl P, Ivarsson A. 1994. Noise-exposed male sheet-metal workers using hearing protectors. A longitudinal study of hearing threshold shifts covering fifteen years. *Scandinavian Audiology*; 23: 123–8.

Caffarella, R.S. 1994. *Planning programs for adult learners: A practical guide for educators, trainers and staff developers.* San Francisco.

Campbell-Lendrum, Concha-Barrientos, M., D., & Steenland, K. (2004). *Occupational noise: assessing the burden of disease from work-related hearing impairment at national and local levels.* Geneva, World Health Organization. (WHO Environmental Burden of Disease Series, No. 9)

Chen J.D. & Tsai J.Y. 2003. Hearing loss among workers at an oil refinery in Taiwan. *Archives of Environmental and Occupational Health*, 58, 55 – 58.

Debra K.Nims. 1999. *Occupational Noise in Basic of Industrial Hygiene* pg. 203-213. U.S.A : Wiley.

Department of Occupational Safety and Health Malaysia. 2006. *Noise Exposure Guidelines*.

Department of Occupational Safety and Health Malaysia. 2010. *Annual Report*.

Department of Occupational Safety and Health Malaysia. 2010. *Estimating Accident Costs in Small Medium Manufacturing Industries in Malaysia*.

Department of Occupational Safety and Health Malaysia. 2011. *OSH Master Plan 2015*.

Dobie R. 2008. The burden of age-related and occupational noise-induced hearing loss in United State. *Ear & Hearing Journal* 29:565–577

Drummond, M.F., Sculpher, M.J., Torrance, G.W., O'Brien, B.J., Stoddart, G.L. 2005. *Methods for Economic Evaluation of Health Care Programmes*. United Kingdom: Oxford University Press

Edwards R, Green W. 1987. Effect of an improved hearing conservation program on earplug performance in the workplace. *Noise Control Engineering Journal*; 28: 55–65

Ezzat S., Aljunid S.M, Zafar A., Saperi S., Amrizal M., 2010. Burden of Disease Associated with Cervical Cancer in Malaysia and Potential Cost and Consequences of HPV Vaccination. *Asian Pacific Journal of Cancer Prevention* 11:1551-1559

Factories and Machinery (Noise Exposure) Regulations.1989. Kuala Lumpur.

Fuente A., Hickson, L., 2011. Noise-induced hearing loss in Asia. *International Journal of Audiology* 50 supp.1(84) : S3-10.

Franks, J.R. and Morata, T.C. 1996. Ototoxic Effects of Chemicals Alone or in Concert with Noise: A Review of Human Studies. *Scientific Basis of Noise-Induced Hearing Loss,* Editors; pages 437-446.New York

Goeree, R., Gafni, A., Hannah, M., Myhr, T. and Blackhouse, G. 1999. "Hospital selection for unit cost estimates in multicentre economic evaluations. Does the choice of hospitals make a difference?", *Pharmacoeconomics*, Vol. 15 No. 6, pp. 561-72.

Goelzer B, Hansen CH, Sehrndt GA, eds. *Occupational exposure to noise: evaluation, prevention and control.* Geneva, World Health Organization, and Dortmund/Berlin, the Federal Institute for Occupational Safety and Health.

Haider M.Y., Taous A., Rahim M., Zaharul Haq A.H.M., Abdullah M. 2008. Noise induced hearing loss among the textile industry workers. *Bangladesh Journal of Otorhinolaryngology* 14(2):39-45.

Hager WL, Hoyle ER, Hermann ER. 1982. Efficacy of enforcement in an industrial hearing conservation program. *American Industrial Hygiene Association Journal*; 43: 455–65

Hetu R, Getty L, Beaudry J, Phflibert L. 1994. Attitudes towards co-workers affected by occupational hearing loss I: Questionnaire development and inquiry. *British Journal of Audiology* 28: 299-3

Lim K.L., Jacobs P., Dewa C. 2008. *How much do we spend on mental health? IHE Report.* Institute of Health Economics.

Lusk, S.L., Ronis, D.L., Kazanis, A.S., Eakin, B.L., Hong, O. & Raymond, D.M. 2003. Effectiveness of a tailored intervention to increase factory workers' use of hearing protection. *Nursing Research*, 52(5), 289-295

Malaysia Standard Industrial Classification (2008).

Ministry of Health Malaysia. 2000, *Criteria for the Diagnosis of Occupational Noise Induced Hearing Loss.*

Ministry of Human Resource, Malaysia. 1991. *Report of the national survey on hearing problems among industry workers.*

Ministry of Human Resource, Malaysia. 2001. Opening speech at the Regional Conference on Occupational Safety and Health. www.l.jaring.my/ksm.

Nasir H.M., Rampal K.G. 2012. Hearing Loss and Contributing Factors Among Airport Workers in Malaysia. *Medical Journal of Malaysia* 67(1):81-6.

National Institute for Occupational Safety and Health (NIOSH). 1998. A proposed national strategy for the prevention of noise-induced hearing loss. *In Proposed national strategies for the prevention of leading work- related diseases*, Part 2 (pp. 51–63).

National Institute for Occupational Health. *Work related hearing loss*. NIOSH Publication No. 2001-103. Available at: http://www.cdc.gov/niosh/ docs/2001-103/. Published 2001.

National Institute of Deafness and Other Communicating Disorders. 2008. *Noise Induced Hearing Loss*. Fact Sheet No: 08-4233.

Neghab M., Maddahi M. & Rajaeefard A.R. 2009. Hearing impairment and hypertension associated with long term occupational exposure to noise. *Iranian Red Crescent Medical Journal*, 11:160 – 165.

Nelson DI, Concha-Barrientos M, Driscoll T, Steenland K, Fingerhut M, Prüss-Üstün A, Corvalan C, Leigh J. 2004. The global burden of disease due to selected occupational risk factors. *American Industrial Hygiene Association Journal*;

Nelson D.I., Nelson R.Y., Concha-Barrientosm M., Fingerhut M. 2005. The global burden of Occupational Noise-Induced Hearing Loss. *American Journal of Industrial Medicine* 48(6):446-458

Ni C.H., Chen Z.Y., Zhou Y., Zhou J.W., Pan J.J. et al. 2007. Associations of blood pressure and arterial compliance with occupational noise exposure in female workers of textile mill. *China Medicine Journal*, 120:1309 – 1313

Noorhassim I, Rampal KG. 1998 Multiplicative effect of smoking and age on hearing impairment. *American Journal of Otolaryngology* 19(4):240-243.

Nor Saleha I.T., Noor Hassim I. 2006. A Study on Compliance to Hearing Conversation Programme among Industries in Negeri Sembilan. *Industrial Health Journal* 44:584-591.

Noweir MH, El-Dakhakhny AA, Valic F. 1968. Exposure to noise in the textile industry of the U.A.R. *American Industrial Hygiene Association Journal* 29(1):541-546. Obiako

Occupational Safety and Health (Notification of Accident, Dangerous Occurrence, Occupational Poisoning and Occupational Disease) Regulations. 2004. Kuala Lumpur.

Palmer K.T., Griffin MJ, Syddall HE, Davis A, Pannett B & Coggon D. 2002.Occupational Exposure to Noise and the Attributable Burden of Hearing difficulties in Great Britain. *Journal of Occupational and Environmental Medicine.* 59: 634-9.

Passchier-Vermeer W. 1993. *Noise and health.* The Hague, Health Council of the Netherlands (Publication No. A93/02E). Prince

R. Dobie. 2008. The burdens of age-related and occupational noise-induced hearing loss in the United States. *Ear and hearing Journal.* 29(4) : 565-77.

Rabinowitz PM, Galusha D, Slade MD et al. (2007) Do ambient noise exposure levels predict hearing loss in a modern industrial cohort? *Occupational and Environment Medicine* 64: 53–9

Savell JF, Toothman EH. 1987. Group mean hearing threshold changes in a noise-exposed industrial population using personal hearing protectors. *American Industrial Hygiene Association Journal*; 48: 23–7

Singh L.P., Bhardwaj A., Deepak K.K., Bedi R. 2009. Occupational Noise Exposure in Small Scale Hand Tools Manufacturing (Forging) Industry (SSI) in Northern India. *Industrial Health Journal* 47:423-430.

Smith, A. 2004. *The fifteenth most serious health problem in the WHO perspective.* Presentation to IFHOH World Congress, Helsinki, July 2004.

Social Security Organization Malaysia. 2011. Annual Report.

South T. 2004. *Industrial Noise in Managing Noise and Vibration at work.* Oxford: Elsevier Butterworth-Heinemann.

Tak S, Davis RR, Calvert GM. 2009. Exposure to hazardous workplace noise and use of hearing protection devices among USworkers-NHANES, 1999–2004. *American Journal of Industrial Medicine* 52:358–71.

Toivonen M, Paakkonen R, Savolainen S et al. 2002. Noise attenuation and proper insertion of earplugs into ear canals. *Annals of Occupational Hygiene* 46: 527–30 van Charante, A.W. M.,& Mulder, P.G.H. 1990. Perceptual acuity and the risk of industrial accidents. *American Journal of Epidemiology,* 121, 652–663

van Kempen EE, Kruize H, Boshuizen HC, Ameling CB, Staatsen BA, de Hollander AE 2002. The association between noise exposure and blood pressure and ischemic heart disease: a meta-analysis. *Environmental Health Perspectives,* 110(3):307–317

Verbeek J. 2007. The Occupational Health Field in the Cochrane Collaboration. *Industrial Health Journal* 45:8-12.

Waitzman N, Smith K. 1998. Unsound conditions: work-related hearing loss in construction, 1960–75. Center to Protect Worker's Rights Washington, DC.

Weston, H. C.,& Adams, S. (1935). *The performance of weavers under varying conditions of noise (*Report No. 70). London:Medical Research Council Industrial Health Research Board.

World Health Organization (WHO). 1995. *Occupational and Community Noise.* World Health Organization.

World Health Organization (WHO). 1999. *Guidelines for community noise.* Edited by Berglund B, Lindvall T, and Schwela DH. Available at http://www.who.int/docstore/peh/noise/guideline s2.html.

World Health Organization (WHO). 2004. *Assessing the burden of disease from work-related hearing impairment at national and local levels.* Environmental Burden of Disease Series No.9, World Health Organization.

Zohar D, Cohen A, Azar N. 1980. Promoting increased use of ear protectors in noise through information feedback. *Human Factors*; 22: 69–79.

APPENDIX A
QUESTIONNAIRES FOR WORKERS (QP)

SENARAI SEMAK PEKERJA
QUESTIONNAIRES FOR RESPONDENT

BEBAN EKONOMI DARI KEHILANGAN PENDENGARAN AKIBAT KEBISINGAN DI MALAYSIA
ECONOMIC BURDEN OF NOISE INDUCED HEARING LOSS IN MALAYSIA

> **PART 1: LATARBELAKANG (*BACKGROUND*)**

Informasi dari Bahagian 1,2 & 3 diperlukan untuk anggaran kes NIHL di Malaysia.

Information from Part 1,2 & 3 will help to estimate the number of NIHL cases in Malaysia.

Nama (*Name*) :_____
Alamat (Address) :_____

Telefon (*Telephone*)   : _____
Tarikh lahir (Date of birth): _____ Umur (Age) : _____
Bangsa (Race)   : Melayu (*Malay*) / Cina *(Chinese)* /
                          India *(India)* / Lain-lain *(Others)*
Jantina (Gender)   : Lelaki (*Male*) / Perempuan *(Female)*
Pendidikan (*Education*) : Rendah (*Primary*) / Menegah
                          (*Secondary*) / Universiti (*University*)
Status Perkahwinan   :Bujang (*Single*) / Berkahwin *(Married)*
(*Marital Status*)
Jawatan (Designation)   :_____
Tarikh mula bekerja
(*Date of start work*)   :_____
Keterangan Kerja (*Job description*) :_____
Kerja Syif (Shift work) :Jumlah jam bekerja semingu: _____

    ☐ Ya (*Yes*)   (*Total working hours a week*)

    ☐ Tidak (*No*)

Gaji asas (*Basic Salary*)   :RM _____
Pendapatan seisi rumah setahun   : RM _____
(*Annual Household income*)

PART 2 :TAHAP PENDENGARAN (HEARING STATUS)

---

1. Adakah anda mengetahui tahap pendedahan kebisingan di tempat kerja?
Do you know the level of noise you are exposed?

    ☐ Ya *(Yes)*.   ☐ Tidak *(No)*

2. Simptom yang pernah anda alami :
The symptom that you had experienced is :

1	2	3	4	5
Berdering di sebelah telinga *Ringing on one ear*	Berdering di dua telinga *Ringing on both ears*	Berasa telinga tersumbat di sebelah telinga *Feeling fullness in one ear*	Berasa telinga tersumbat di dua telinga *Feeling fullness in both ears*	Sukar memahami percakapan di tempat awam *Difficult to understand speech in a crowd*

PART 3 : RAWATAN PERUBATAN (*MEDICAL CARE*)

Maklumat dari Part 3 diperlukan untuk anggaran kos ditanggung oleh pekerja untuk rawatan dan pemulihan NIHL.

Information from Part 3 will help to estimate the cost borne by employee for treatment and rehabilitation of NIHL.

3. Setelah mendapat keputusan Ujian Audiometrik, adakah anda dirujuk ke Pakar Telinga?
upon receiving Audiometric Report, would you referred to any ENT Specialist?

   ☐   Ya *(Yes)*.   ☐   Tidak *(No)*

4. Nyatakan nama, lokasi dan masa rawatan di KLINIK / HOSPITAL PAKAR:
*State name, location and time spend at the **SPECIALIST CLINIC/HOSPITAL**:*

Bil	Nama & lokasi klinik / Hospital Name& location of Clinic/Hospital	Masa Rawatan (jam) Duration time spend (hours)	Jenis Rawatan (Type of care)	Jumlah Yuran Rawatan Medical Care Fee (RM)
1			A, B, C	
2			A, B, C	

Pilih Jenis Rawatan Pakar (Notes for Type of Specialist Care) di bawah :
Choose type of medical care you by the ENT Specialist as below:

    A : Ujian audiometrik *(Audiometric test)*
    B : Pembedahan Koklea *(Cohclear Implant)*
    C : Rundingcara dan pemuliharaan *(Consultation & Rehabilitation)*

5. Adakah sebarang ubat-ubatan diberikan selepas rawatan pakar?
What are the medication prescribed by the specialist doctor after the treatment?

    ☐ Ya *(Yes)*.   ☐ Tidak *(No)*

6. Semasa rawatan pakar, adakah anda disarankan menggunakan alat bantu dengar?
Do the ENT Specialist recommend hearing aid?

    ☐ Ya *(Yes)*.   ☐ Tidak *(No)*

Jenis alat bantu dengar *(Type of hearing aid):* _____

Sila ke soalan 8. (Proceed to no.8)

7. Adakah anda mebayar harga alat bantu dengar yang disarankan?
Do you pay for the hearing aid recommended by the Specialist?

☐ Ya *(Yes).*
Nyatakan jumlah bayaran (*state amount paid*) RM
_____

☐ Tidak *(No)*

8. Pada hari rawatan, adakah doktor pakar memberi anda sijil cuti sakit?
Do you get sick leave upon the specialist medical care?

☐ Ya *(Yes).*
hari *(days)*

☐ Tidak *(No)*

PART 4 : RAWATAN ALTERNATIF (*ALTERNATIVE CARE*)

---

9. Selain dari rawatan perubatan, adakah anda mencuba rawatan alternatif untuk masalah pendengaran? *Have you undergone any alternative treatment due to hearing problem?*

☐ Ya *(Yes).* ☐ Tidak *(No)*

10. Pilih Jenis Rawatan Alternatif yang dijalankan (*Notes for Type of Alternative Care*) :

- Perubatan Tradisional Cina : Akupuntur, teh herba dan urutan *(Tradisional Chinese Medicine - Acupunture, herbal tea and massage.)*
- Rawatan Ayuverdic (Ayurverdic Treatment)
- Perubatan Islam Ruqyah (Quranic verse treatment)
- Makanan tambahan (*Special food/beverage*)
- Ubatan herbal (*Herbal medication*)

11. Kekerapan mendapatkan rawatan *(Frequency of treatment)*:

___

12. Jumlah perbelanjaan rawatan *(Alternative Care Cost)* : RM

___

PART 5 : PENGANGKUTAN SEMASA RAWATAN (*TRANSPORTATION FOR TREATMENT*)

Maklumat dari Part 5 membantu anggaran kos pengangkutan semasa rawatan dan pemuliharaan NIHL.
Information from Part 5 will help to estimate the cost of ransportation for treatment and rehabilitation of NIHL.

Jumlah kos pengangkutan (Total transportation cost)	Rawatan Perubatan *Medical Care*	Pakar Telinga *ENT Specialist*	Rawatan Alternatif *Alternative Care*
Kenderaan Sendiri *Own Transport*	RM	RM	RM
Kenderaan awam *Public Transport*	RM	RM	RM

PART 6 : PENJAGA / AHLI KELUARGA (*CARE GIVER*)

Maklumat dari Part 6 membantu anggaran kos ditanggung oleh penjaga/ahli keluarga pekerja semasa rawatan dan pemuliharaan NIHL.

Information from Part 6 will help to estimate the burden of caregiver during treatment and rehabilitation of NIHL.

13. Adakah anda ditemani oleh ahli keluarga semasa mendapatkan rawatan perubatan / alternatif?
Do your family member accompany you for medical / alternative care?

☐ Ya *(Yes)*.   ☐ Tidak *(No)*

14. Ahli keluarga yang menenami anda mempunyai kerjaya?
Do your family member a career person?

☐ Ya *(Yes)*.
Nyatakan jumlah pendapatan sebulan *(Monthly salary)*:
RM _____

☐ Tidak *(No)*
Tidak bekerja *(Not working)*

PART 7: TAHUN PRODUKTIVITI (PRODUCTIVE YEARS)

Maklumat Part 7 diperlukan bagi pekerja yang MASIH BEKERJA walaupun mengalami NIHL. Jika tidak lagi bekerja sila ke soalan 17.

The following questions are referred to the workers that **STILL WORKING** after having hearing loss. If no longer working, answer question 17.

15. Pernahkah anda dipindahkan ke seksyen kerja yang lain?
Were you being removed from the previous job?

- ☐ Ya *(Yes)*.
- ☐ Tidak *(No)*

16. Adakah perpindahan berkenaan menyebabkan gaji anda dikurangkan?
Was there salary reduction upon removal?

- ☐ Ya *(Yes)*. Jumlah pendapatan sebulan *(Monthly salary)*: RM _____
- ☐ Tidak bekerja *(Not working)*

Maklumat di bawah merujuk kepada pekerja YANG TIDAK LAGI BEKERJA setelah mendapat NIHL.
The following questions are referred to the worker that has **NO LONGER WORKING** *after having hearing loss.*

17. Adakah anda diberhentikan kerja disebabkan mendapat NIHL?
Were you being terminated from the previous job due to hearing loss?

- ☐ Ya *(Yes)*. Berapa gaji terakhir (Last salary before termination): RM _____
- ☐ Tidak *(No)*

19. Berapa lamakah anda telah diberhentikan kerja?
_____bulan

How many months have you been terminated?

20. Bagaimana anda menjana pendapatan keluarga setelah diberhentikan?

How do you generate family income after being terminated?

- Berniaga sendiri (Own business)
- Bertani & menternak (agriculture)
- Bekerja di tempat lain (Working in other organization)

Terima kasih di atas maklumbalas. Semoga tuan/ puan sekeluarga sentiasa dirahmati.
Thank you for your response. May you and your family be blessed always.

APPENDIX B

QUESTIONNAIRES FOR EMPLOYERS (QE)

SENARAI SEMAK MAJIKAN
QUESTIONNAIRES FOR EMPLOYER

BEBAN EKONOMI DARI KEHILANGAN PENDENGARAN AKIBAT KEBISINGAN DI MALAYSIA
ECONOMIC BURDEN OF NOISE INDUCED HEARING LOSS IN MALAYSIA

PART 1: LATARBELAKANG (*BACKGROUND*)

Informasi dari Bahagian 1,2 & 3 diperlukan untuk anggaran kes NIHL di Malaysia.
Information from Part 1,2 & 3 will help to estimate the number of NIHL cases in Malaysia.

Nama Syarikat :_____
(Name of organization)

Alamat Syarikat :_____
(Address of organization)

Telefon (*Telephone*):_____ Faksimili (*Facsimiles*): _____

Klasifikasi Industri (*Industrial Classification*):_____

PART 2: WAKIL MAJIKAN (*EMPLOYER'S REPRESENTATIVE*)

Nama (*Name*):_____
Jawatan (*Designation*): Pegawai Keselamatan dan Kesihatan (SHO) /_____
Tarikh mula bekerja (*Date of start work*): _____
Jantina (*Gender*) :_____

PART 3: PENGURUSAN PENDEDAHANBUNYI BISING (*NOISE EXPOSURE MANAGEMENT*)

Sila tanda (/) pada jawaban yang bersesuaian dan isi tempat kosong.
For questions below, kindly tick (/) at relevant answer and fill in the blanks.

Adakah majikan mengendalikan Ujian Audiometrik ke atas pekerja yang terdedah kepada bunyi pada / melebihi paras bertindak ?
Do employer conduct the Audiometric Test for the workers whom exposed to noise at / more than action level?

☐ Ya (*Yes*). ☐ Tidak (*No*)
Tarikh Ujian Audiometrik asas dijalankan
(*Date of baseline audiometric test conducted*)

_____

2. Adakah majikan menjalankan ujian audiometrik setiap tahun?
Do employer conduct audiometric test every year?

☐ Ya (*Yes*). ☐ Tidak (*No*)
Tarikh Ujian Audiometrik tahun lalu
(*Date of baseline audiometric test last year*)

_____

3. Dari laporan pemonitoran bunyi bising, bilangan pekerja yang terdedah kepada tahap kebisingan lebih dari 85dB:
From the noise monitoring (mapping), state the number of workers exposed to noise more than 85dB:

- **Bilangan pekerja terdedah:** _____
  (*No. of exposed workers*)

- **Bilangan pekerja keseluruhan:** _____
  (*Total number of workers*)

4. **Dari laporan Audiometrik, nyatakan bilangan pekerja yang mempunyai masalah pendengaran pada tahun 2011:**
From the audiometric report, state number of workers having hearing problem on 2011 :

- *Hearing impairment:* _____
- *Hearing loss at higher frequency:* _____
- *Profound Hearing loss:* _____

5. **Adakah majikan membekalkan alat perlindungan telinga kepada pekerjanya?**
Do employer provide hearing protection device to the workers?

    ☐ Ya (*Yes*).   ☐ Tidak (*No*)
    Nyatakan jenis perlindung telinga dibekalkan
    (*Type of ear protections provided were*) _____

6. **Adakah majikan menyediakan program latihan berkaitan pendedahan bising kepada pekerja termasuk penyesuaian pelindung telinga ?**
Do employer provide training program for the workers including attenuation of hearing device?

    ☐ Ya (*Yes*).   ☐ Tidak (*No*)

PART 4 : STATUS PENDEDAHAN BISING
(***NOISE EXPOSURE STATUS***)

Tandakan jawaban yang sesuai. (*Kindly tick suitable answer*).

11. Berapa peratus dari jumlah pekerja terdedah kepada persekitaran kerja yang bising melebihi 85 dbA?
What is the percentage of *workers expose to noisy working environment more than 85dBA?*

<u>1</u>	<u>2</u>	<u>3</u>	<u>4</u>	<u>5</u>
5 %	20 %	50 %	80 %	100%

12. Tahap pendedahan bising di tempat kerja adalah
The level of noise at your workplace is:

<u>1</u>	<u>2</u>	<u>3</u>	<u>4</u>	<u>5</u>
0 – 65 dBA	66 – 80 dBA	81 - 85 dBA	86 - 90 dBA	90 - 140 dBA

PART 5 : RAWATAN PERUBATAN (*MEDICAL CARE*)

Maklumat dari Part 5 diperlukan untuk anggaran kos ditanggung oleh majikan untuk rawatan dan pemulihan NIHL.
Information from Part 5 will help to estimate the cost borne by employer for treatment and rehabilitation of NIHL.

13. Berdasarkan laporan audiometrik, majikan merujuk pekerja yang mengalami NIHL ke Pakar ENT di
Based on audiometric report, employer referred workers with NIHL to ENT Specialist at

- ☐ Hospital Kerajaan (*Government Hospital*)
- ☐ Pusat Perubatan Swasta (*Private Medical Centre*)

14. **Purata bayaran perkhidmatan perubatan oleh Pakar ENT bagi setiap pekerja? RM** _____
Average service cost by the ENT Specialist per worker?

15. **Purata kos alat bantu dengar yang dicadangkan oleh Pakar ENT bagi setiap pekerja? RM** _____
Total cost for the hearing aid proposed by the ENT Specialist?

16. **Majikan menyediakan penyenggaraan bateri alat bantu dengar secara berkala?**
Employer provide regular battery maintenance for the hearing aid?

- ☐ Ya (*Yes*)
  Nyatakan jumlah bayaran (*state amount paid*)
  RM _____

- ☐ Tidak (*No*)

- ☐ Tidak berkenaan
  (Not applicable)

17. **Adakah bayaran premium insuran pekerja meningkat setelah rawatan diberi?**
Was the premium insurance payment of the organization increase after treatment of employees?

- ☐ Ya (*Yes*)
  Nyatakan jumlah bayaran (*state amount paid*)
  RM _____

- ☐ Tidak (*No*)

- ☐ Tidak berkenaan
  (Not applicable)

Maklumat dari Part 6 membantu anggaran kos pengangkutan yang ditanggung majikan semasa rawatan dan pemuliharaan NIHL.
Information from Part 6 will help to estimate the cost of transportation for treatment and rehabilitation of NIHL.

18. Adakah majikan menyediakan pengangkutan kepada pekerja untuk mendapatkan rawatan / pemuliharaan?
Do employer provide transportation for the employees to get treatment/rehabilitation?

☐ Ya (*Yes*)   ☐ Tidak (*No*)
Nyatakan purata kos setiap pekerja
(average cost per worker)
RM _____

19. Kekerapan menghantar pekerja bagi mendapatkan rawatan NIHL pada 2011: _____ kali
Frequency of transport usage for medical care due to NIHL in 2011:

PART 7: KERUGIAN PRODUKTIVITI (*PRODUCTIVITY LOSS*)

Maklumat dari Part 7 membantu anggaran kerugian produktiviti ditanggung oleh syarikat.
Information from Part 7 will help to estimate the production loss of the company.

20. Adakah berlaku penurunan kadar pengeluaran apabila pekerja dengan NIHL mendapatkan rawatan?
Were there a reduction of production due to workers with NIHL went for treatment?

☐ Ya (*Yes*)
Nyatakan kadar pengeluaran sebelum rawatan
(*state* production rate - before treatment)
RM _____

☐ Tidak (*No*)

☐ Tidak berkenaan (Not applicable)

21. Adakah terdapat kelewatan penghantaran produk semasa pekerja menjalani rawatan?
Are there any delays of product delivery due to workers with NIHL go for treatment?

☐ Ya (*Yes*)

☐ Tidak (*No*)

☐ Tidak berkenaan (Not applicable)

22. Adakah syarikat didenda akibat kelewatan atau pembatalan tempahan?
Did the company being fine for the delay or cancelation?

☐ Ya (*Yes*)
Nyatakan jumlah denda (*state amount paid*)

☐ Tidak (*No*)

☐ Tidak berkenaan (Not applicable)

23. **Adakah pekerja lain/ penyelia menggantikan pekerja dengan NIHL mendapatkan rawatan?**
Were there any temporary replacement while the workers with hearing loss went for medical care?

  ☐ Ya (*Yes*)   ☐ Tidak (*No*)
  Nyatakan jumlah
  pekerja pengganti
  (*state number of replacement*)
  _____

24. **Adakah pekerja dengan NIHL perlu bekerja lebih masa selepas mendapatkan rawatan?**
Are workers with NIHL need to work overtime after medical care?

  ☐ Ya (*Yes*)   ☐ Tidak (*No*)
  Nyatakan jumlah
  jam bekerja lebih
  masa
  (*state of total overtime hours*)
  _____

25. **Adakah majikan melaksanakan pemindahan perubatan akibat penyakit NIHL ?**
Does your organization implement medical removal due to NIHL?

☐ Ya (*Yes*)　　　　　　　☐ Tidak (*No*)
Nyatakan
bilangan pekerja
(*state of number*
of workers)

_____

Nyatakan jumlah　　　☐ Tidak berkenaan
bayaran upah　　　　　(Not applicable)
pekerja
(*state total wages*)
RM _____

26. Latihan kepada pekerja baru apabila pemindahan perubatan dilaksanakan?
Training for new workers were conducted in the implementation of medical removal?

☐ Ya (*Yes*)　　　　　　　☐ Tidak (*No*)
Nyatakan
bilangan pekerja
(*state of number*
of workers)

_____

　　　　　　　　　　　　　☐ Tidak berkenaan
Nyatakan jumlah　　　(Not applicable)
kos latihan
pekerja baru
(*state total training*
cost)
RM _____

Terima kasih di atas maklumbalas. Semoga tuan/puan sekeluarga sentiasa dirahmati.
Thank you for your response. May you and your family be blessed always.

APPENDIX C
INFORMATION SHEET

| NOTA MAKLUMAT PEKERJA |

Tempat kerja anda telah tersenarai dan anda telah terpilih untuk menyertai kajian penyelidikan ini. Sebelum anda membuat sebarang keputusan, adalah penting anda mengetahui sebab penyelidikan ini dilaksanakan dan apa yang terlibat di dalam kajian ini. Sila baca maklumat berikut dengan teliti.

Tajuk Kajian

BEBAN EKONOMI DISEBABKAN HILANG PENDENGARAN AKIBAT KEBISINGAN DI MALAYSIA

Pengenalan

Bunyi bising di tempat kerja adalah sejenis bahaya yang boleh dicegah tetapi sehingga kini kesedaran terhadap beban ekonomi yang ditanggung masih rendah di kalangan negara membangun termasuk Malaysia. Faktor risiko kebisingan di tempat kerja yang meluas telah menyebabkan pekerja menghidap hilang pendengaran akibat kebisingan di tempat kerja (NIHL). Oleh kerana, risiko ini dikaitkan dengan tempat kerja, justeru majikan dan pekerja perlu menggalas tanggungjawab masing-masing bagi mencegah penyakit pekerjaan ini melanda.

Apakah tujuan kajian dilakukan?

Kajian ini bertujuan untuk mengukur beban ekonomi yang ditanggung akibat menghidap NIHL dari tiga (3) perspektif; pekerja, majikan dan kerajaan. Kajian ini juga bertujuan untuk membuat anggaran jumlah pekerja yang mungkin terdedah kepada NIHL di Malaysia. Kajian ini akan lengkap setahun dari masa pengedaran senarai semak.

Apa dan siapa yang terlibat di dalam kajian ini?

Responden dipilih secara rawak di kalangan pekerja yang disahkan menghidap NIHL berdasarkan senarai kes yang disiasat oleh Jabatan Keselamatan dan Kesihatan Pekerjaan (JKKP). Anda dikehendaki menjawab senarai semak berhubung kos ke atas beberapa perbelanjaan termasuk rawatan dan rehabilitasi NIHL, kos pengangkutan, orang yang menjaga/ menemani semasa rawatan dan bilangan hari tidak bekerja. Sebahagian data akan diperolehi dari pegawai keselamatan dan kesihatan /wakil majikan. Semua data berkaitan kos dibelanjakan oleh pekerja akan direkod dan dianalisa.

Faedah ke atas kajian ini.

Dengan terlaksana kajian ini, pihak pembuat polisi dapat menentukan kos yang ditanggung oleh pekerja yang menderita akibat NIHL. Maklumat yang didapati sangat berguna kepada pembuat polisi untuk meningkatkan penguatkuasaan Program Pemuliharaan Pendengaran (Hearing Conservation Program) di negara ini. Bukan sekadar itu sahaja, analisa kos NIHL juga akan menjadi model dalam menentukan beban ekonomi ke atas penyakit pekerjaan yang lain.

Adakah sebarang risiko sekira menyertai kajian ini?

Tidak. Ini kerana senarai semak ini disusun mengikut format ringkas dan menggunakan ayat yang mudah difahami. Senarai semak ini tidak akan memberi kesan psikologi ke atas responden.

Kerahsiaan

Semua maklumat yang didapati dari senarai semak semasa kajian dijalankan adalah sulit dan dirahsiakan. Hasil keputusan dari maklumat yang terkumpul akan dilaporkan secara bersepadu tanpa merujuk kepada individu tertentu.

Adakah saya perlu menyertai kajian ini?

Penyertaan kajian ini adalah sukarela. Sekiranya anda mengambil bahagian di dalam kajian ini, anda akan diberi nota maklumat ini untuk disimpan. Anda juga diperlukan untuk menandatangan borang persetujuan tetapi jika anda memilih tidak mengambil bahagian, ia tidak menjejaskan hak anda dari segi undang-undang.

Bolehkah saya tarik diri dari kajian ini?

Ya. Responden boleh menarik diri dari kajian ini pada bila-bila masa dengan memaklumkan kepada penyelidik bertugas.

Semakan kajian

Kajian ini akan disemak oleh Sekretariat Penyelidikan Perubatan dan Inovasi, Universiti Kebangsaan Malaysia.

Adakah sebarang bayaran dikenakan?

Tiada sebarang bayaran dikenakan dan tiada bayaran akan diberi kepada responden yang mengambil bahagian di dalam kajian ini.

Maklumat lanjut, sila hubungi :

Noraita Binti Tahir
Penyelidik Kajian
Universiti Kebangsaan Malaysia & United Nation University International Institute of Global Health (UNU-IIGH)
Universiti Kebangsaan Malaysia Medical Centre
Kuala Lumpur

Phone / Fax. No. : 03 - 9145 6685

Terima kasih di atas kerjasama anda.

INFORMATION SHEET FOR WORKERS

Your industries are chosen to take part in a research study. Before you decide, it is important for you to understand why the research is being done and what it will involve. Please take time to read the following information carefully.

Research Title

ECONOMIC BURDEN OF NOISE INDUCED HEARING LOSS IN MALAYSIA

Introduction

Occupational noise is a preventable disease but there is still lack of awareness on the economic burden of the condition in many developing countries including Malaysia. The widespread risk factor of occupational noise impacted an outcome of Noise induced hearing loss (NIHL). Since the risk is associated with the workplace, therefore the employers as well as the employees were to hold the responsibilities.

What is the aim of the study?

The study aimed to measure the economic burden of NIHL and prevalence of NIHL among workers in Malaysia at three perspectives; the patient, the private and the government. This study will be completed in one year and six months from the distribution of questionnaires.

What would this involve?

Patients will be chosen randomly among those workers diagnosed with NIHL based on the list of investigated cases by Department of Occupational Safety and Health (DOSH). You will need to answer a set of questionnaire related to how much do you spend for a few item; treating and rehabilitating of NIHL; transportation fees; who are the person who cared for you and how many days of your work loss. Some of the data will be obtained from your employer. All data of cost borne by the patient will be recorded and analyze.

The benefits

By doing this study we could effectively determine the cost borne by the patient when they suffer from NIHL. The information we get from this study will guide the policy maker to improve the hearing conservation program in the country. Not only that, the cost analysis model will become a template to determine economic burden of other occupational diseases in this country.

The risks

The questionnaire is drafted in a simple format and easy to understand which will not give any psychological effect to the patient.

Confidentiality

All information which is collected about you during the course of the research will be kept strictly confidential. The result of the data obtained will be reported in a collected manner with no reference to a specific individual.

Do I have to take part?

The participation into this study is voluntary. If you do decide to take part you will be given this information sheet to keep and be asked to sign a consent form. But, if you prefer not to take part, you do not have to give reason and your decision will not affect your legal rights.

The right to withdraw

Patient has the right to withdraw from the study at any time by informing the point of the study.

The review of study

The study will be reviewed by the Medical Research and Innovation Secretariat, Universiti Kebangsaan Malaysia.

Payment and compensation

You do not have to pay for participating in this study. Similarly, no payment is available to you for participating in this study.

Contacts for Further Information

If I have any questions, kindly contact point of study below:

Noraita Binti Tahir

United Nation University

International Institute of Global Health (UNU-IIGH)
Universiti Kebangsaan Malaysia Medical Centre
Kuala Lumpur

Phone / Fax. No. : 03 - 9145 6685

Thank you for taking part in this study

APPENDIX D

CONSENT FORM

| BORANG KEBENARAN RESPONDEN |
| CONSENT FORM FOR RESPONDEND |

Tajuk Kajian
Research Title

Beban Ekonomi terhadap Hilang Pendengaran akibat Kebisingan di Malaysia
Economic burden of Noise Induced Hearing Loss in Malaysia

Nama Penyelidik
Name of Researchers

1. Prof. Dato' Dr Syed Mohamed AlJunid
2. Prof. Dr Jamal Hisham Hashim
3. Noraita Binti Tahir

✓ Saya mengesahkan bahawa saya telah membaca dan memahami maklumat di dalam Nota Maklumat

Pekerja untuk tujuan kajian di atas dan berpeluang untuk bertanya soalan kepada penyelidik.
I confirm that I have read and understand the information sheet for the above study and have had the opportunity to ask questions

✓ Saya memahami bahawa penglibatan saya di dalam penyelidikan ini adalah sukarela dan saya boleh menarik diri pada bila-bila masa tanpa alasan dan tiada kesan ke atas hak sebagai pekerja.
I understand that my participation is voluntary and that I am free to withdraw at any time, without giving any reason, without my legal rights being affected

✓ Saya bersetuju untuk mengambil bahagian di dalam kajian ini.
I agree to take part in the above study

Nama responden (*Name*) :
No. K. Pengenalan (*I.C. No*) :
Tarikh (*Date*) :
Tandatangan (*Signature*) :

Nama Penyelidik (*Name of Researcher*) :
Tarikh (*Date*) :
Tandatangan (*Signature*) :

www.ingramcontent.com/pod-product-compliance
Lightning Source LLC
Chambersburg PA
CBHW030755180526
45163CB00003B/1036